THE EXQUISITE COLORING BOOK

ANIMALS

I0499850

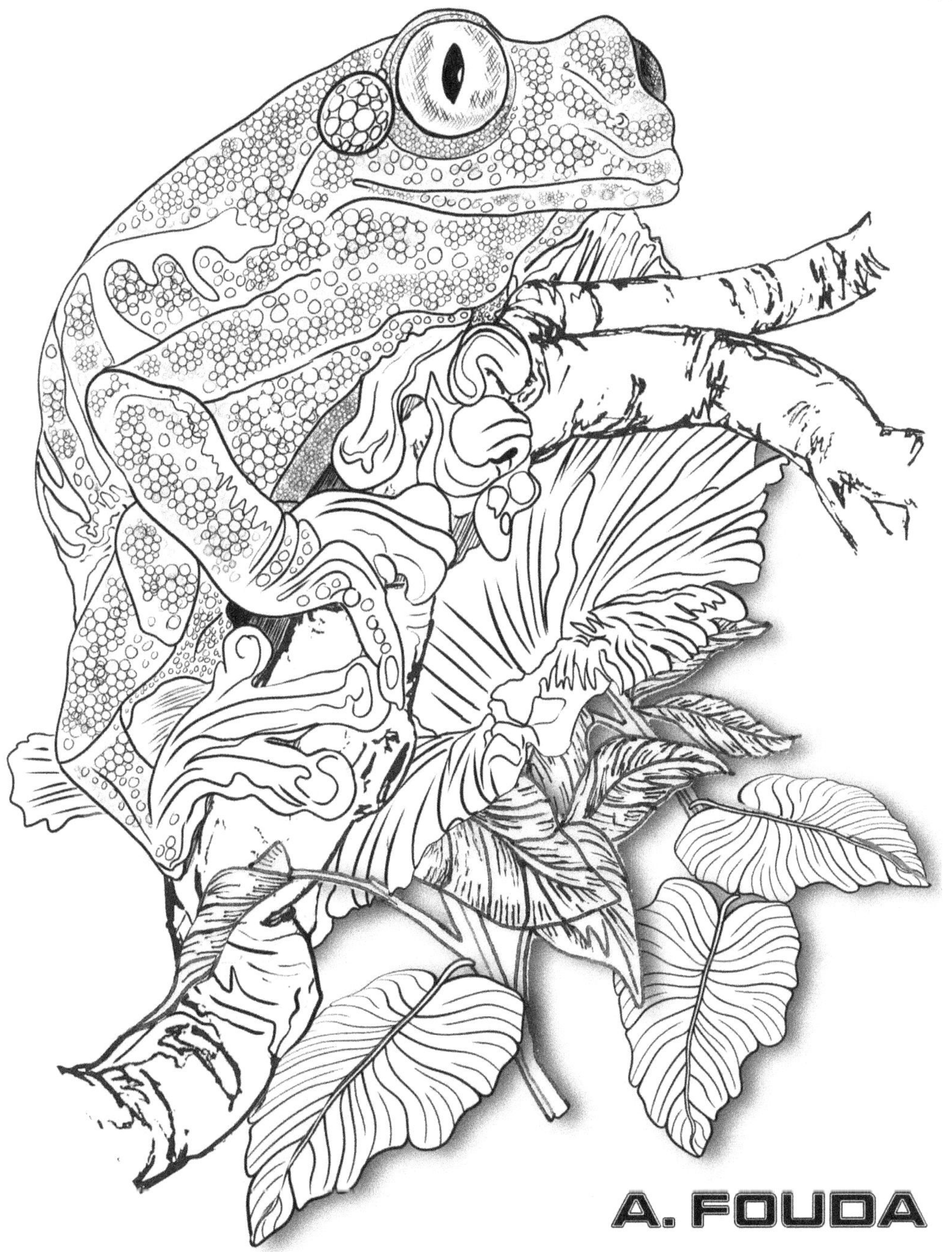

A. FOUDA

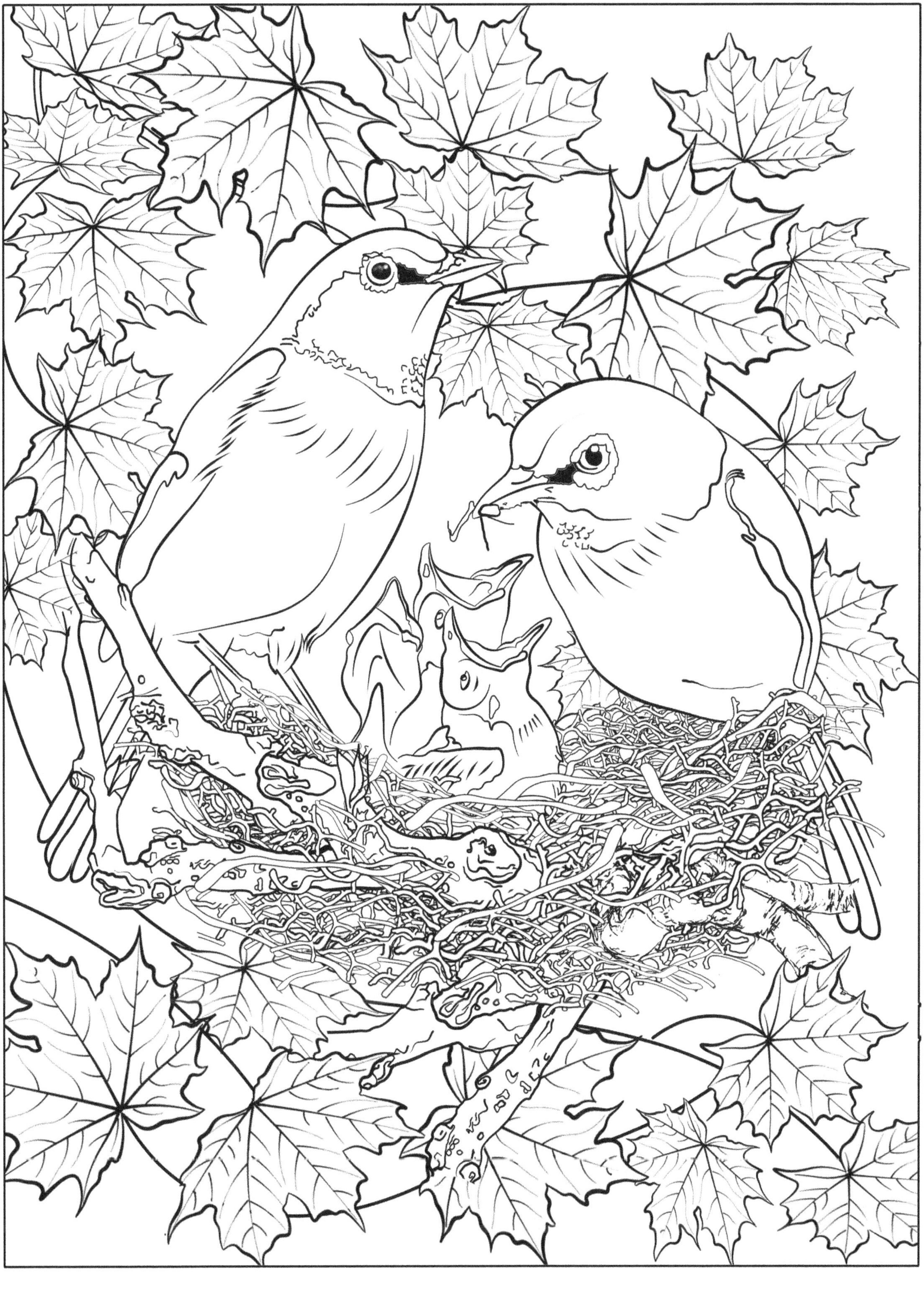

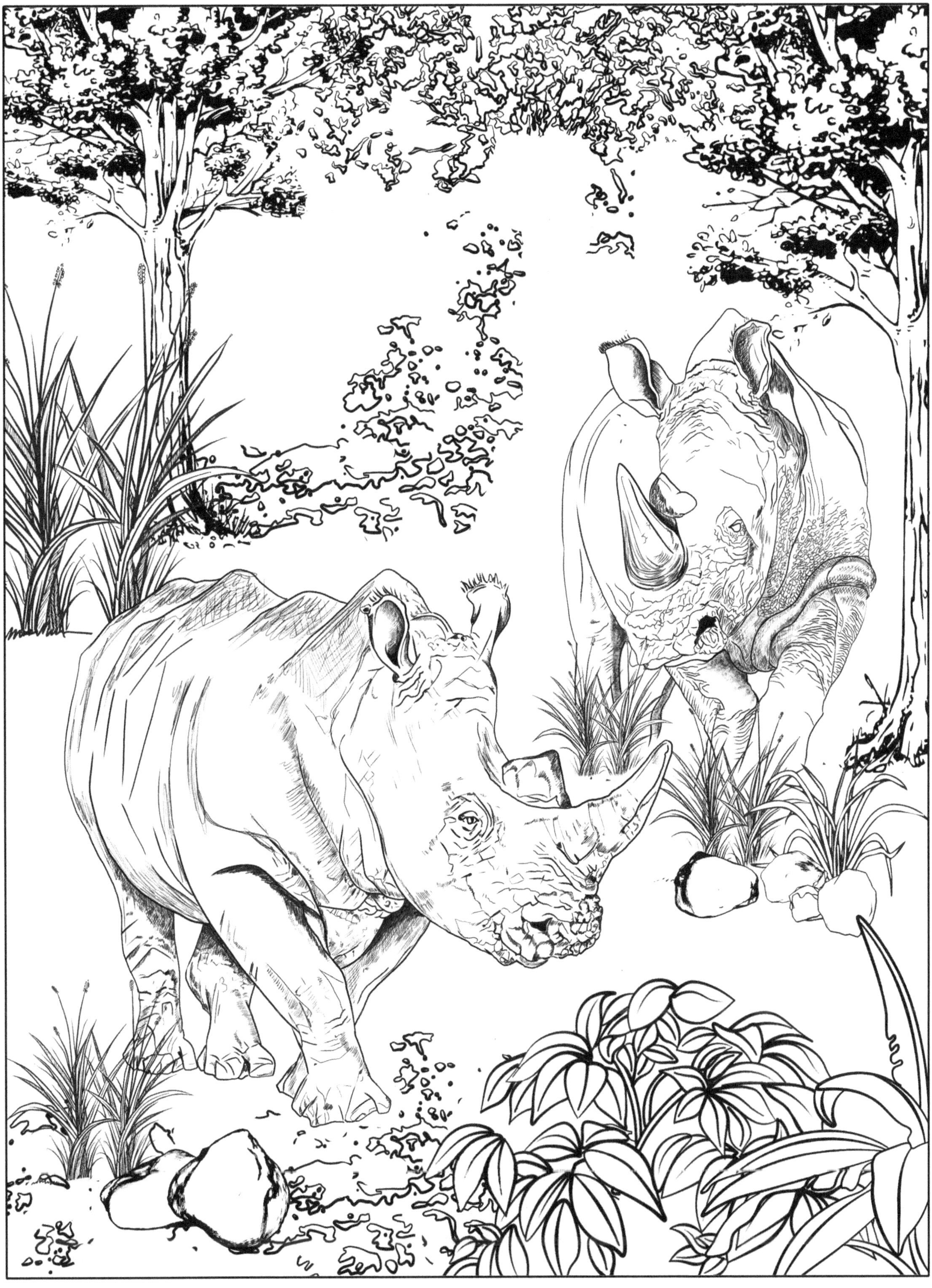

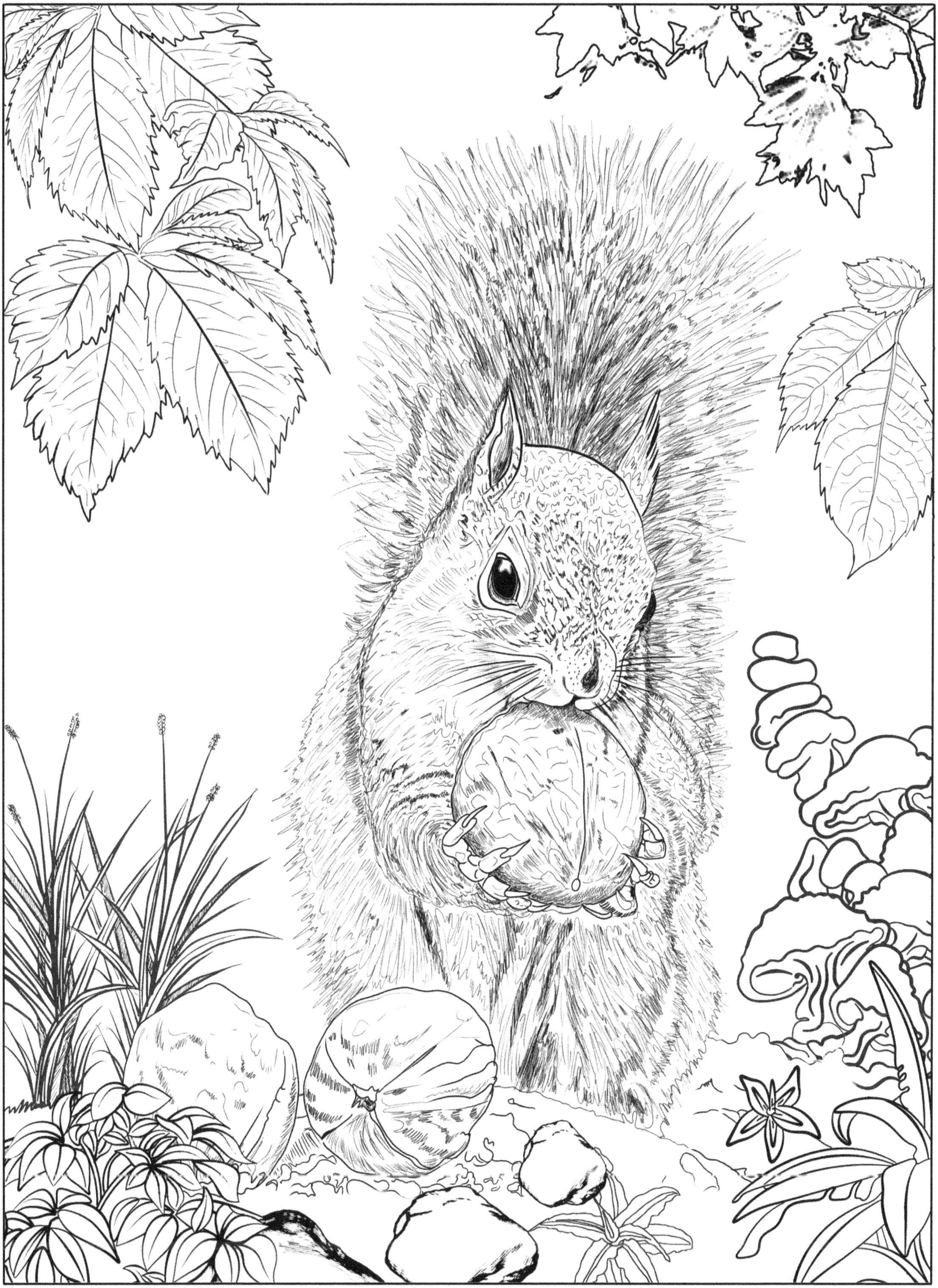

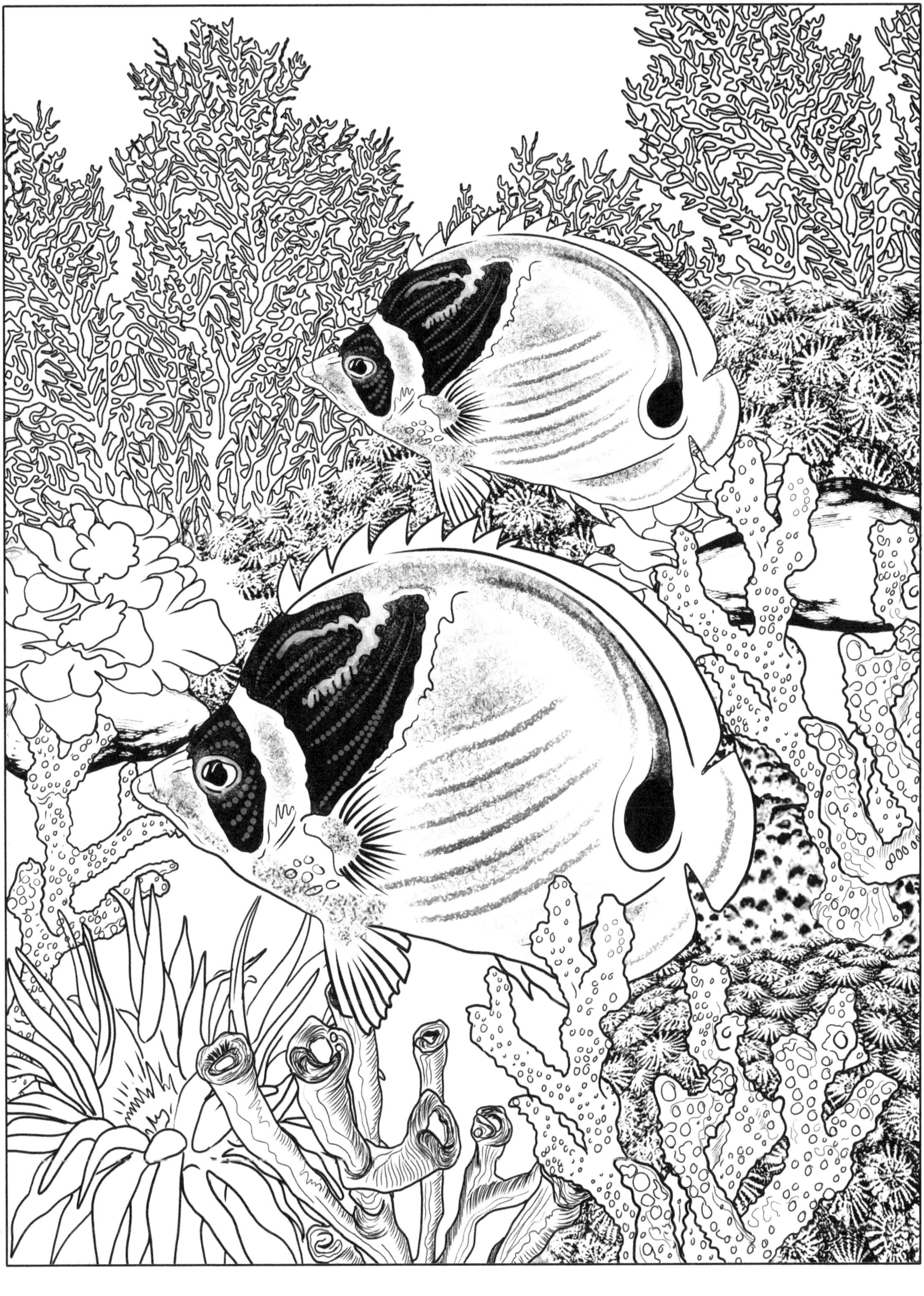

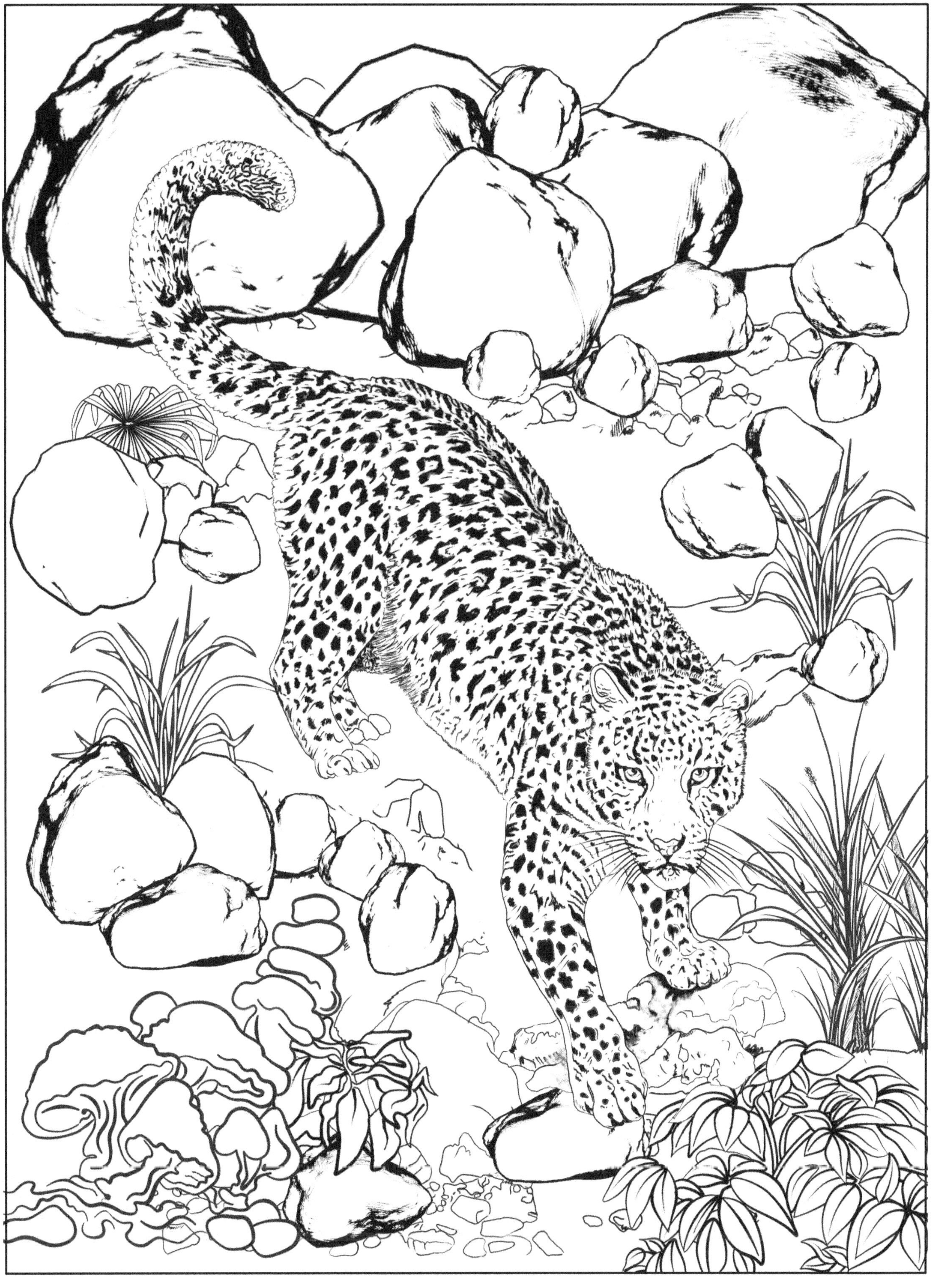

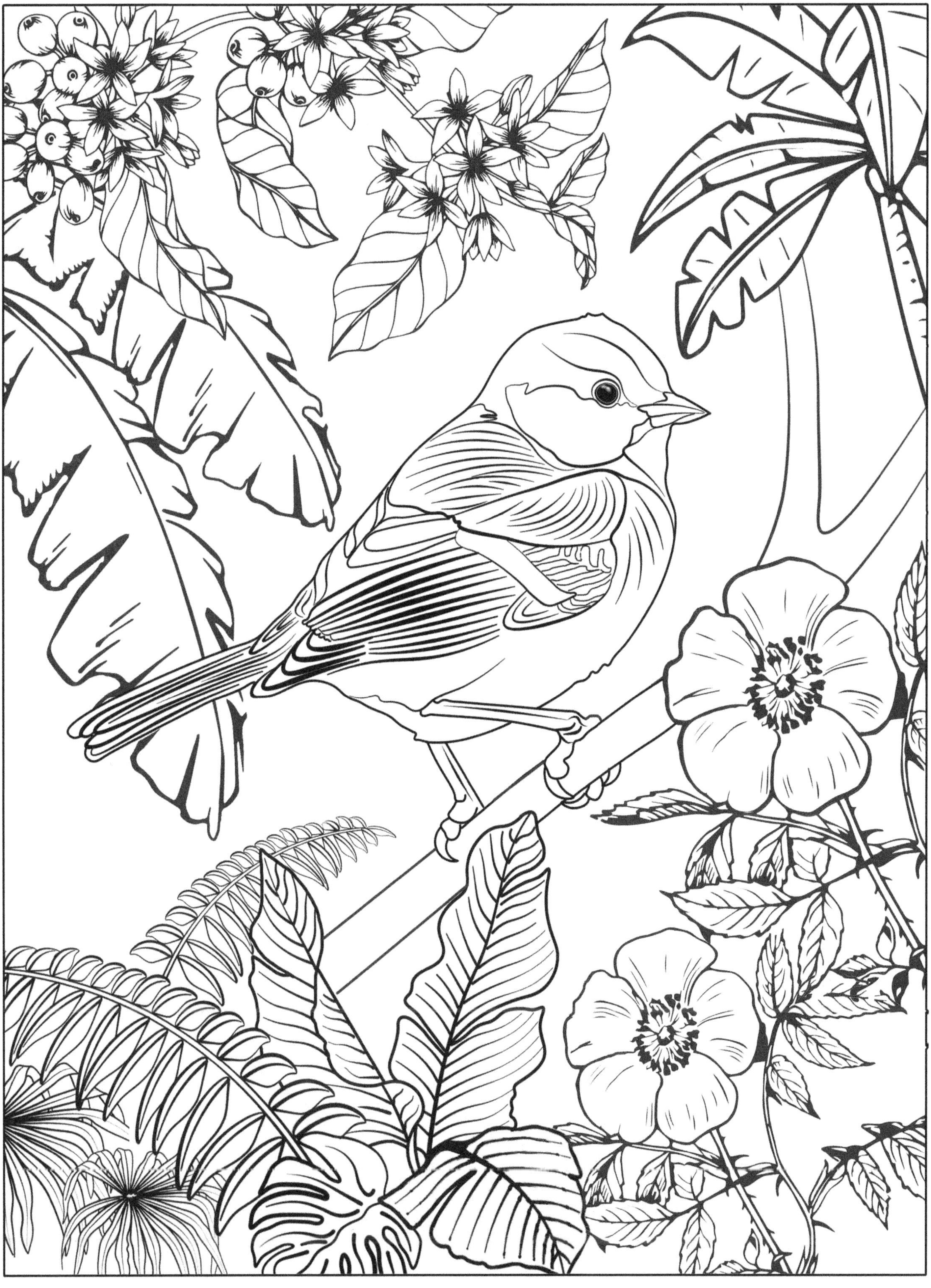

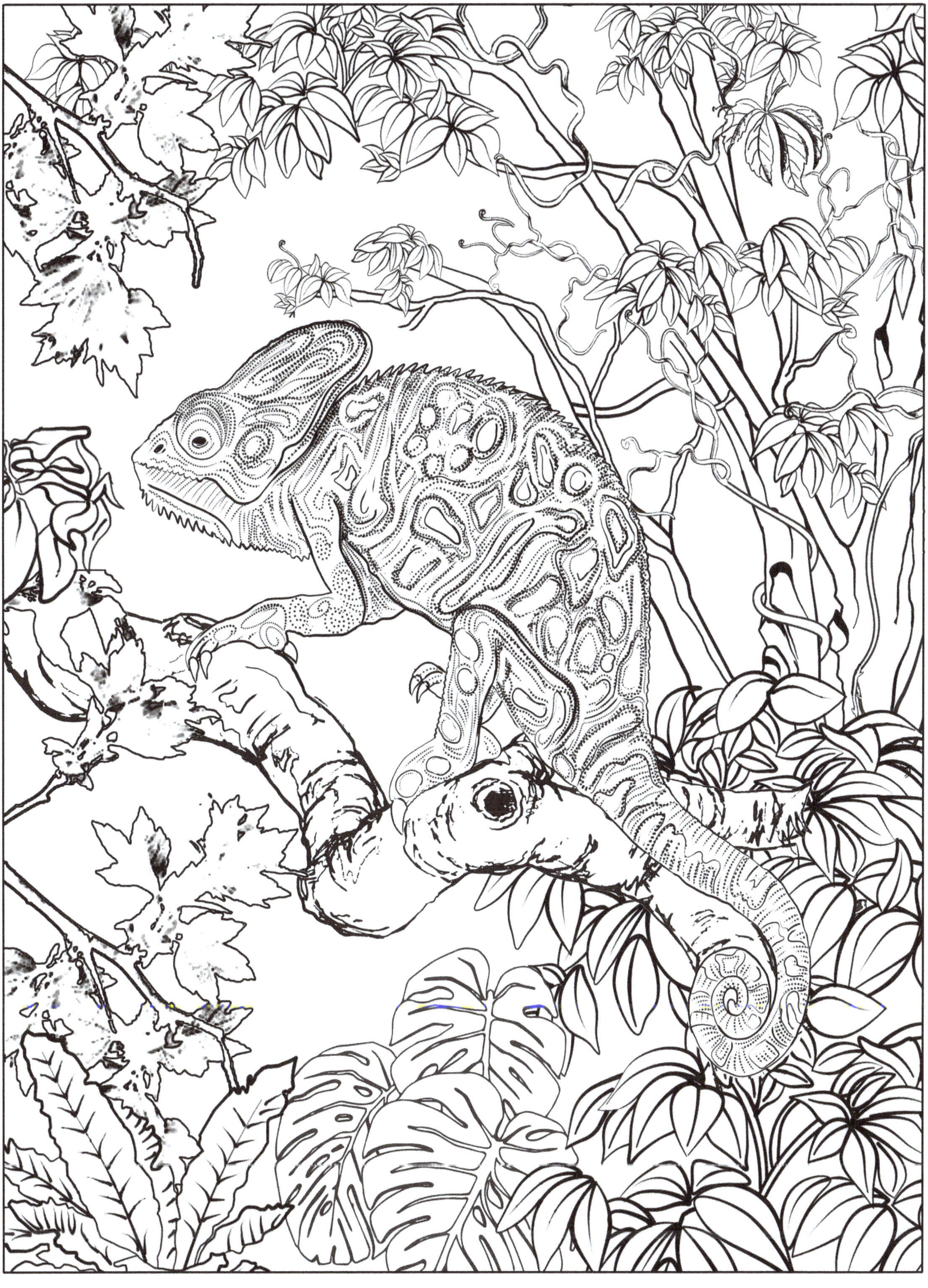

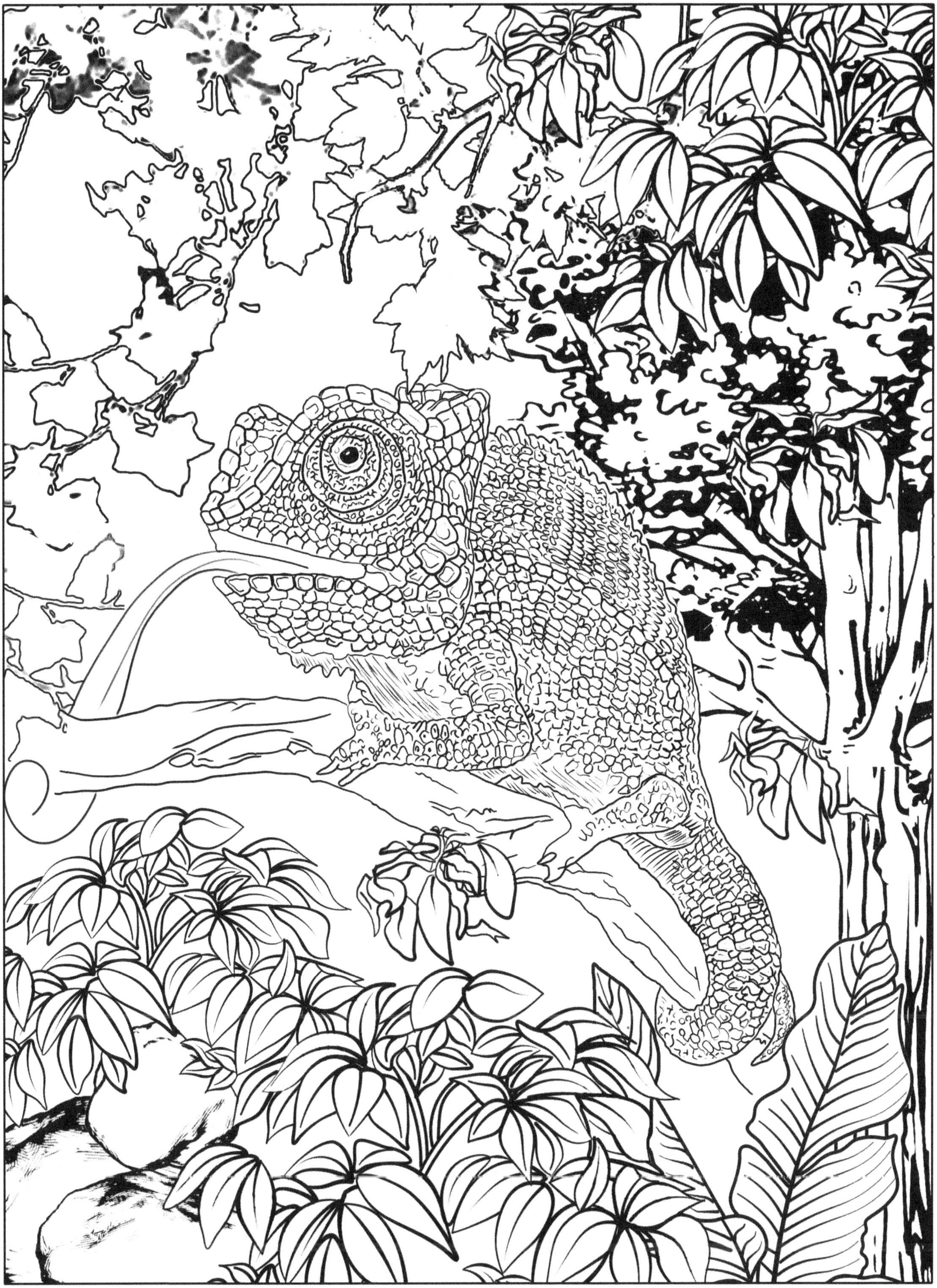

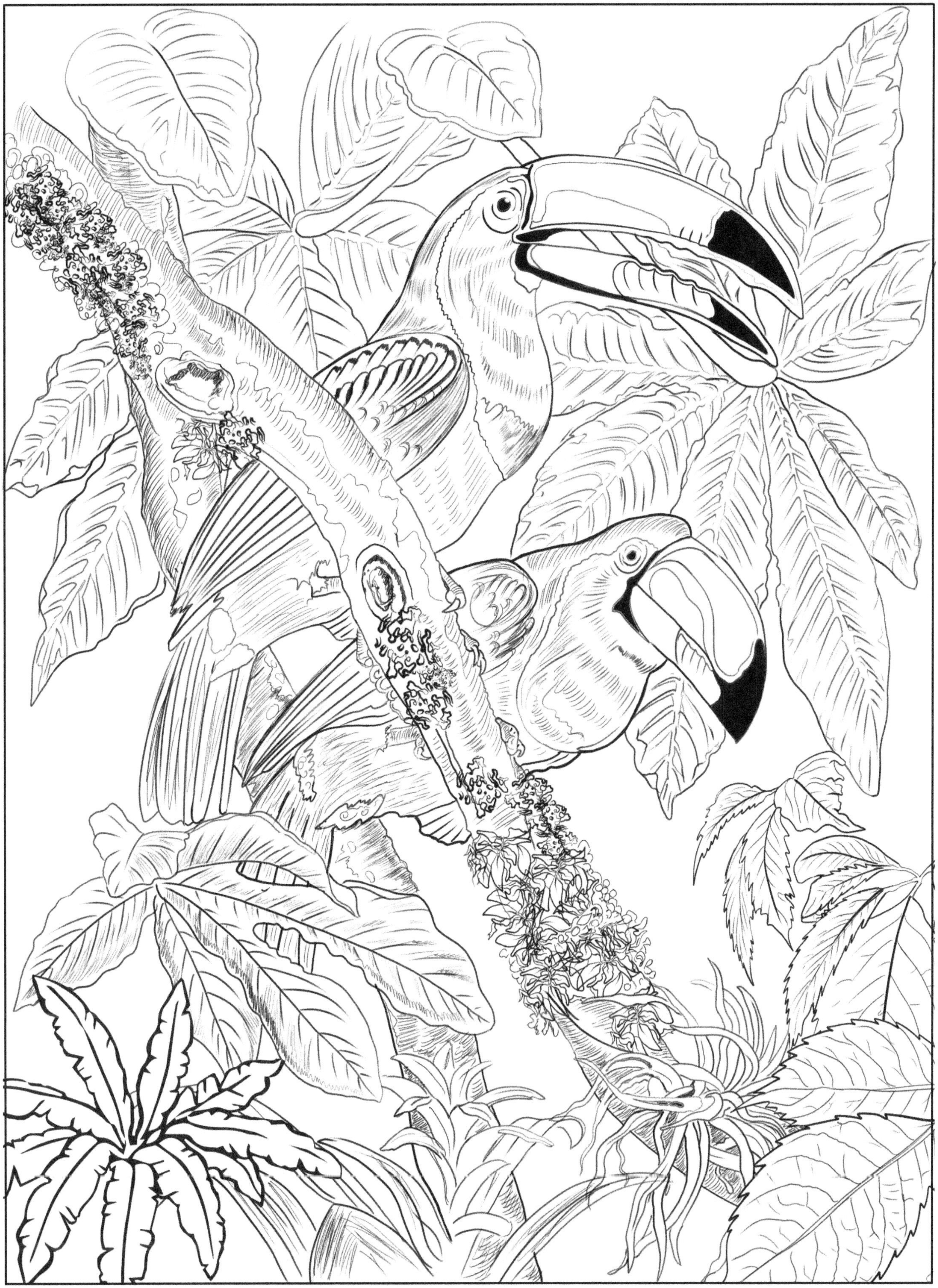

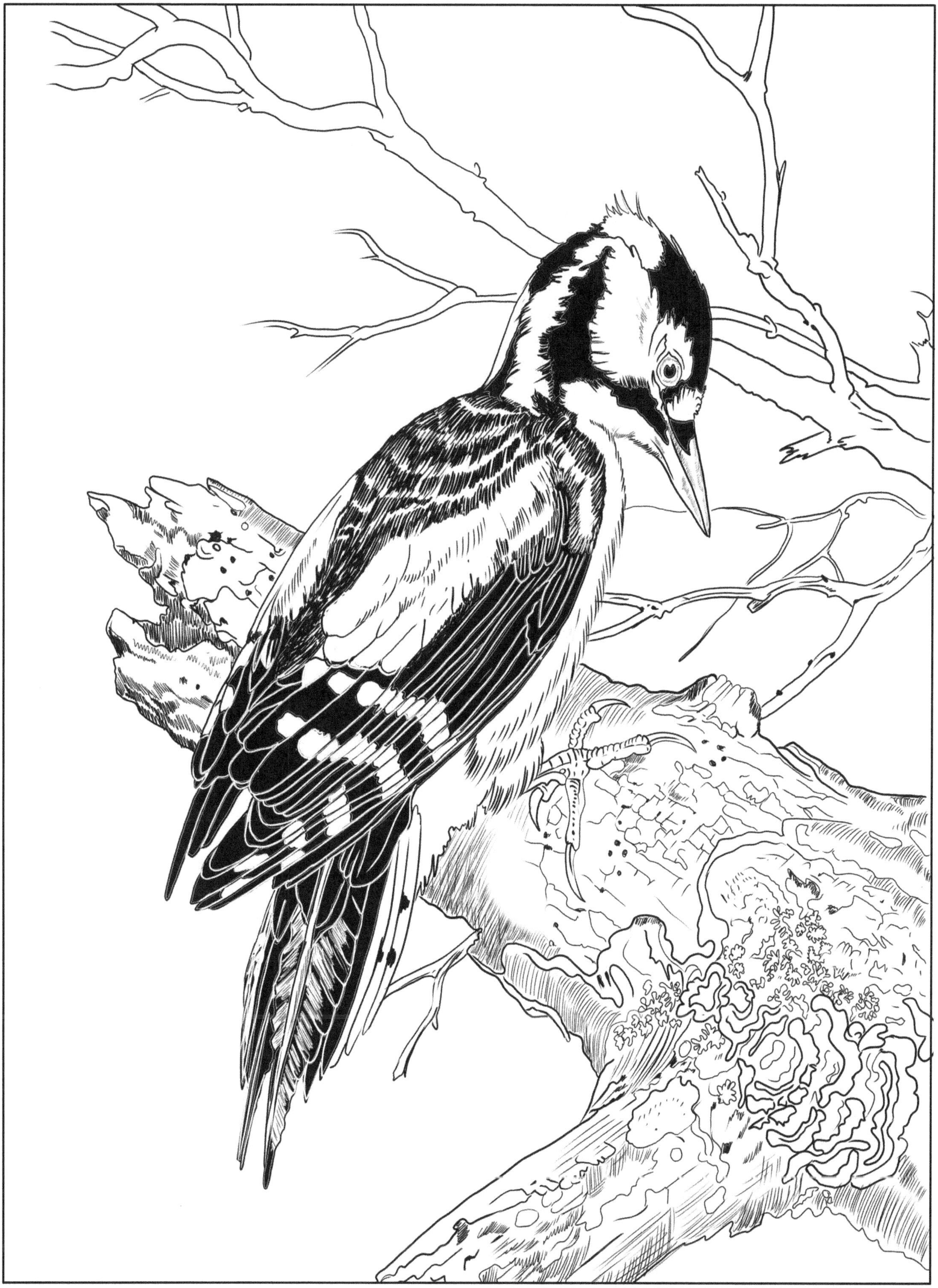

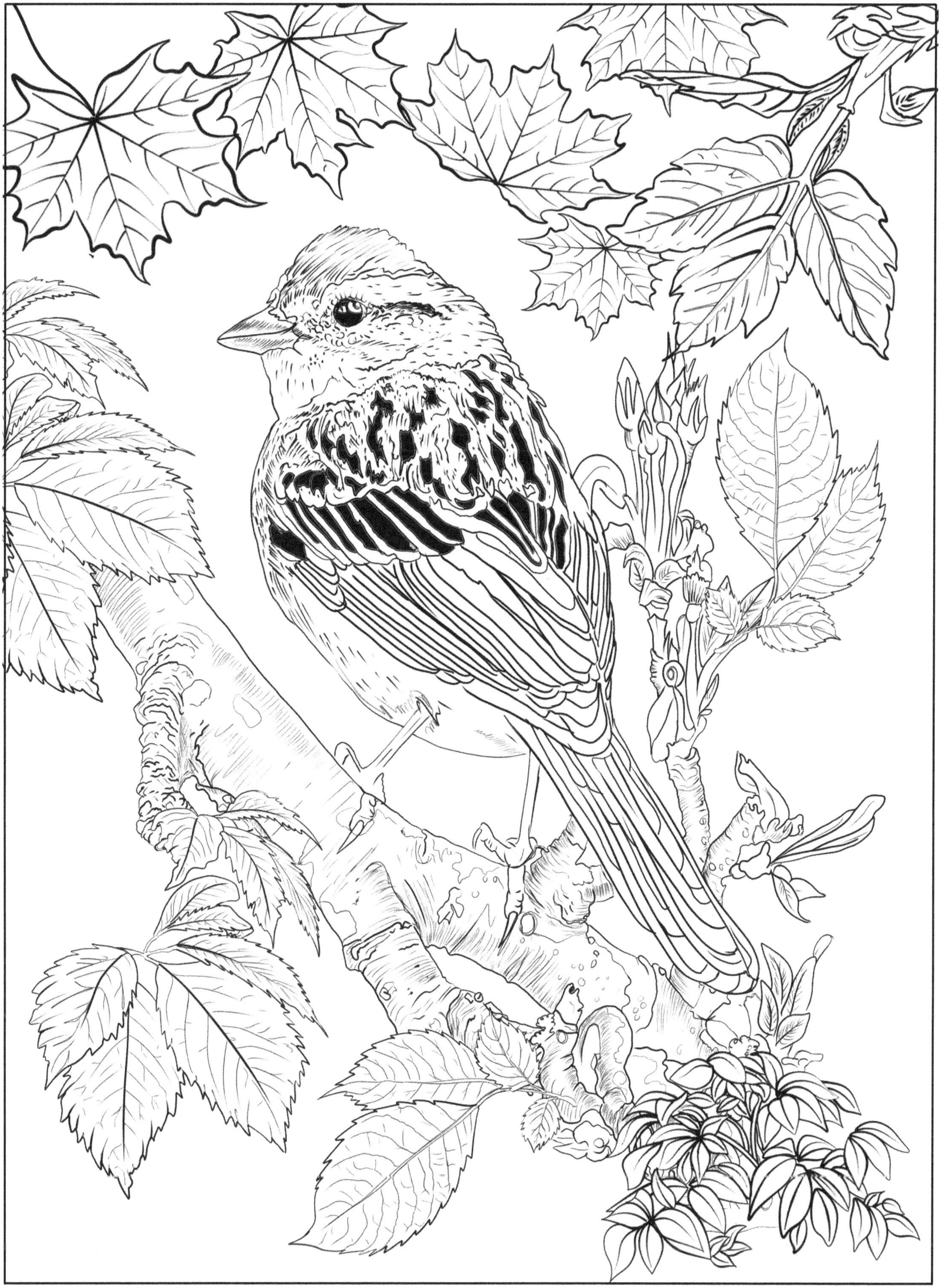

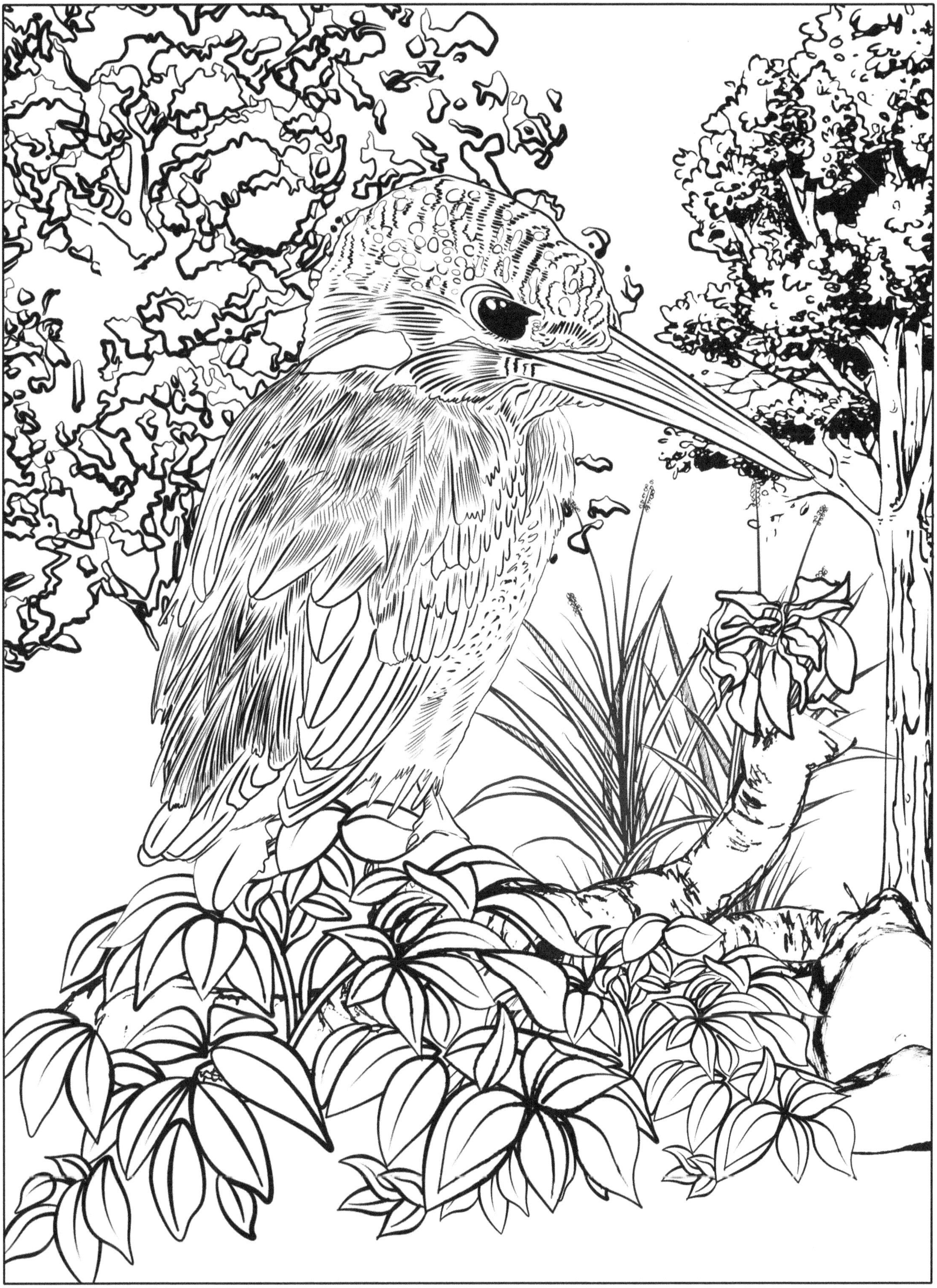

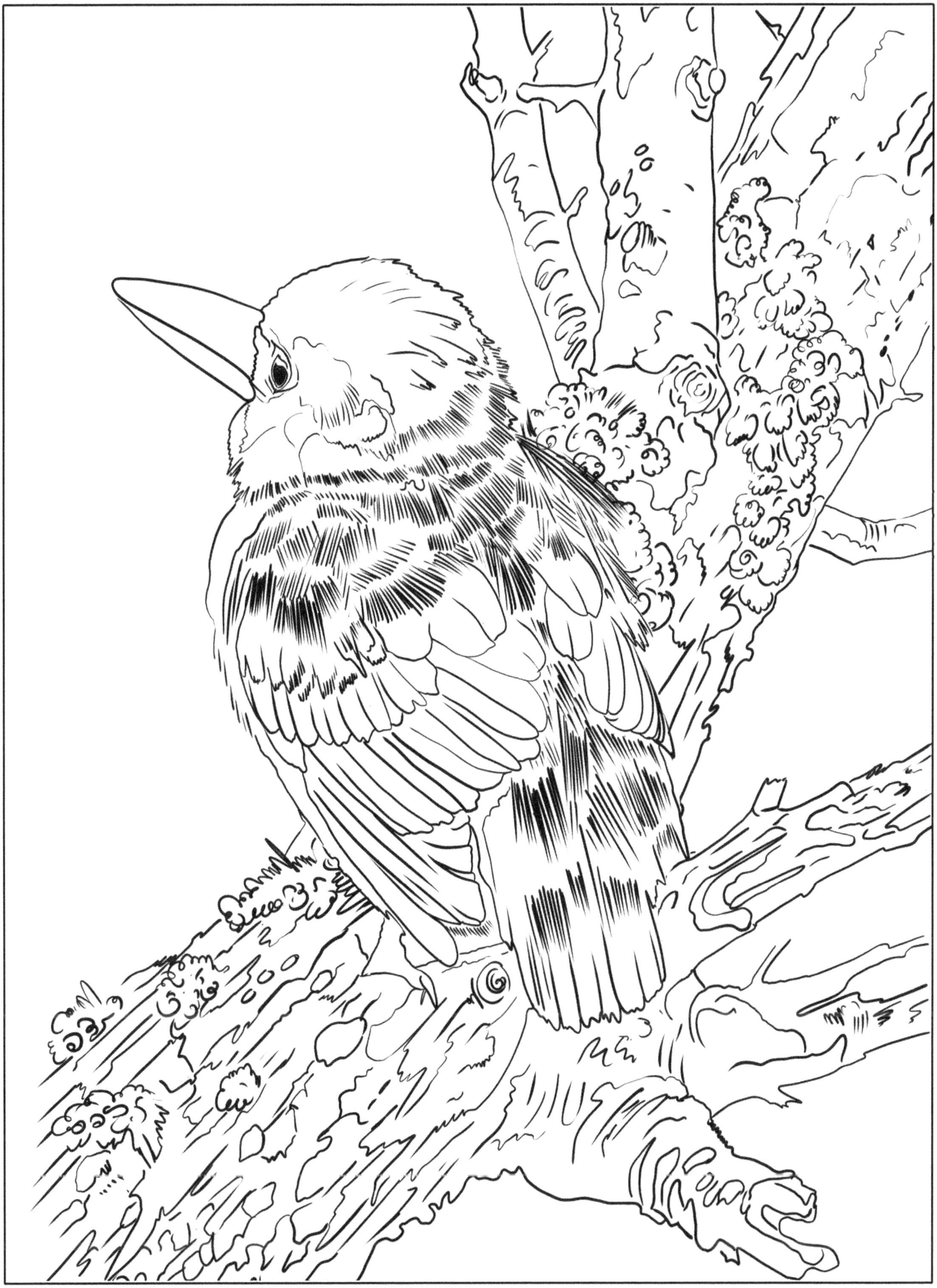

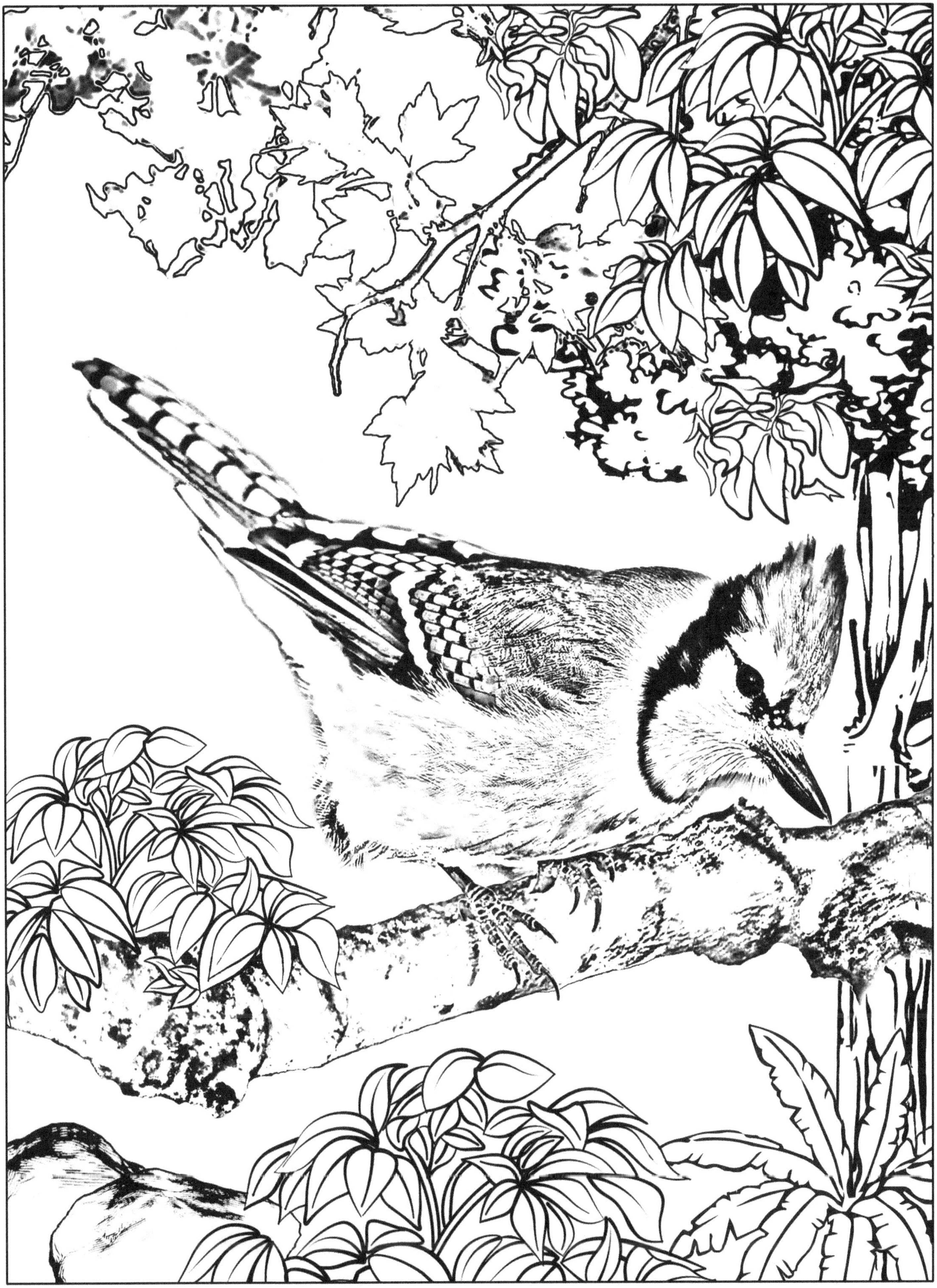

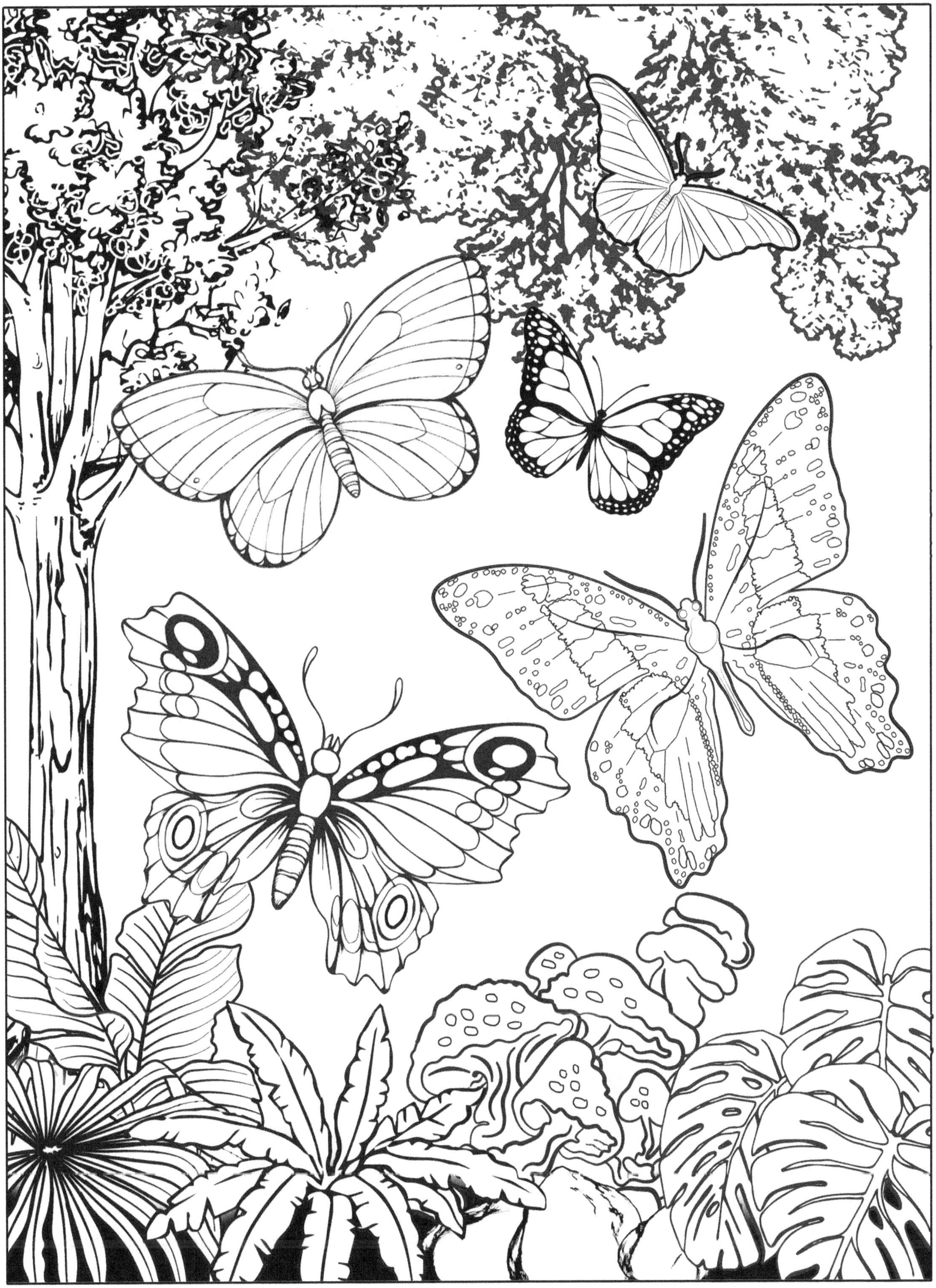

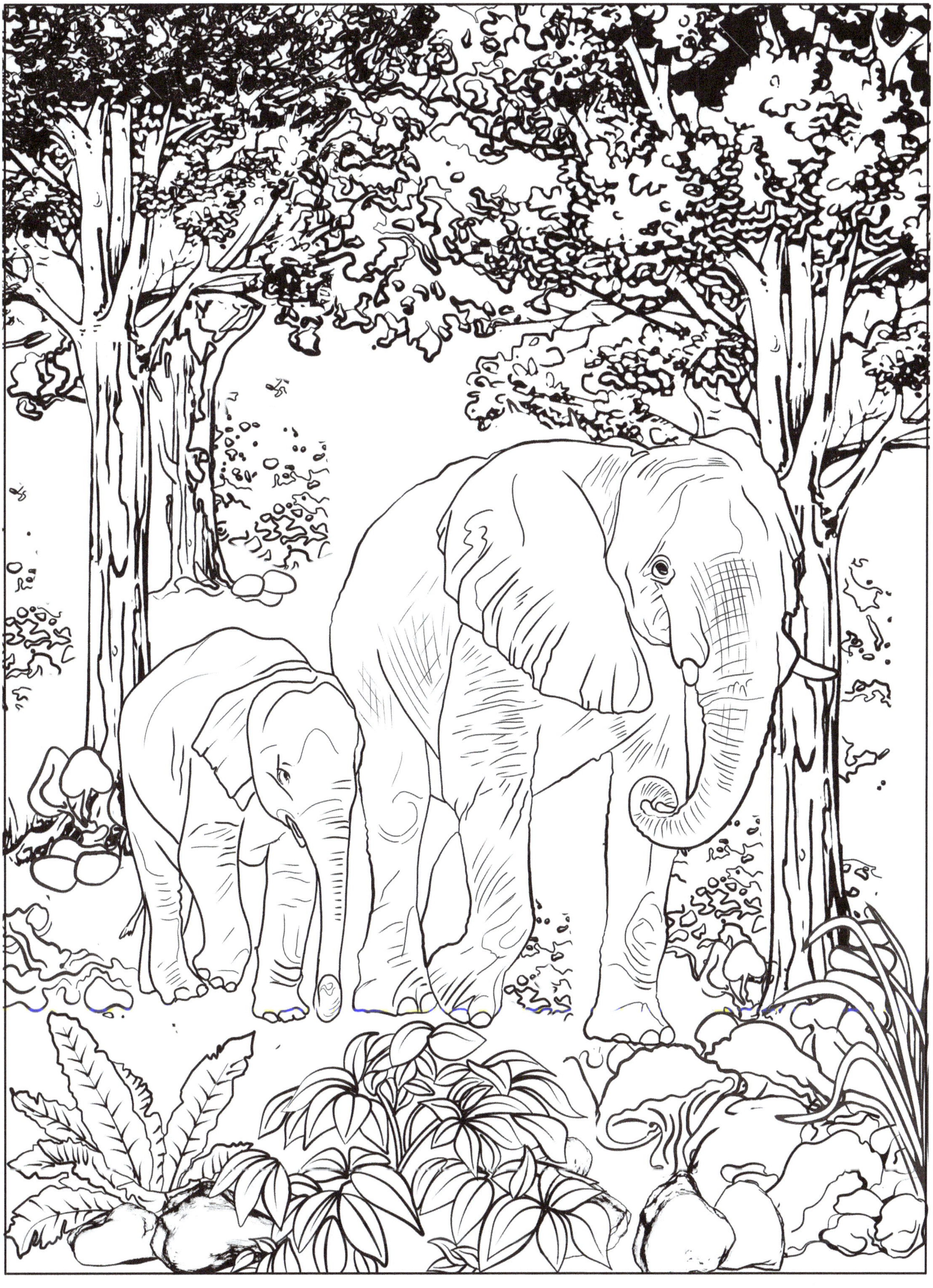

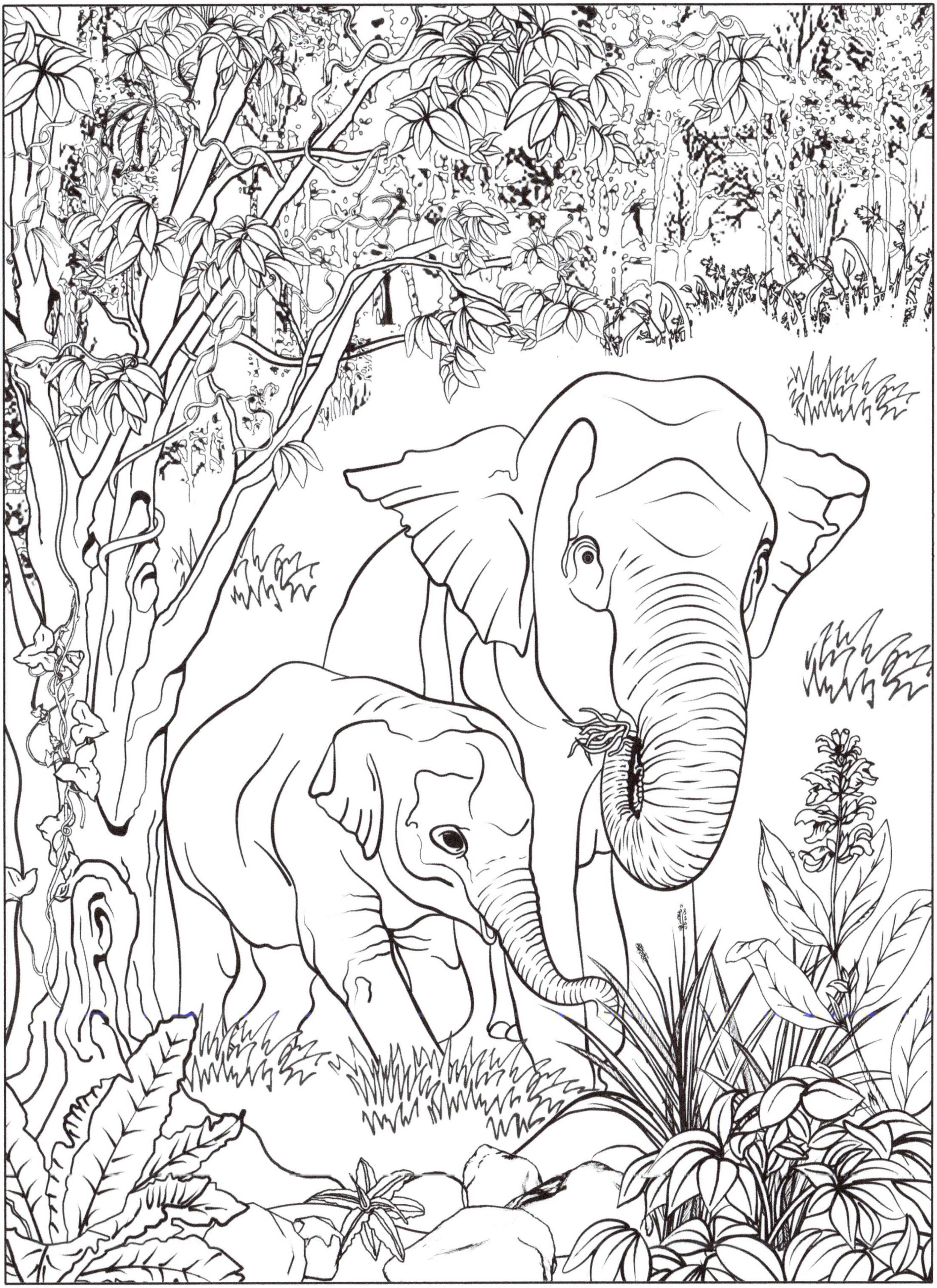

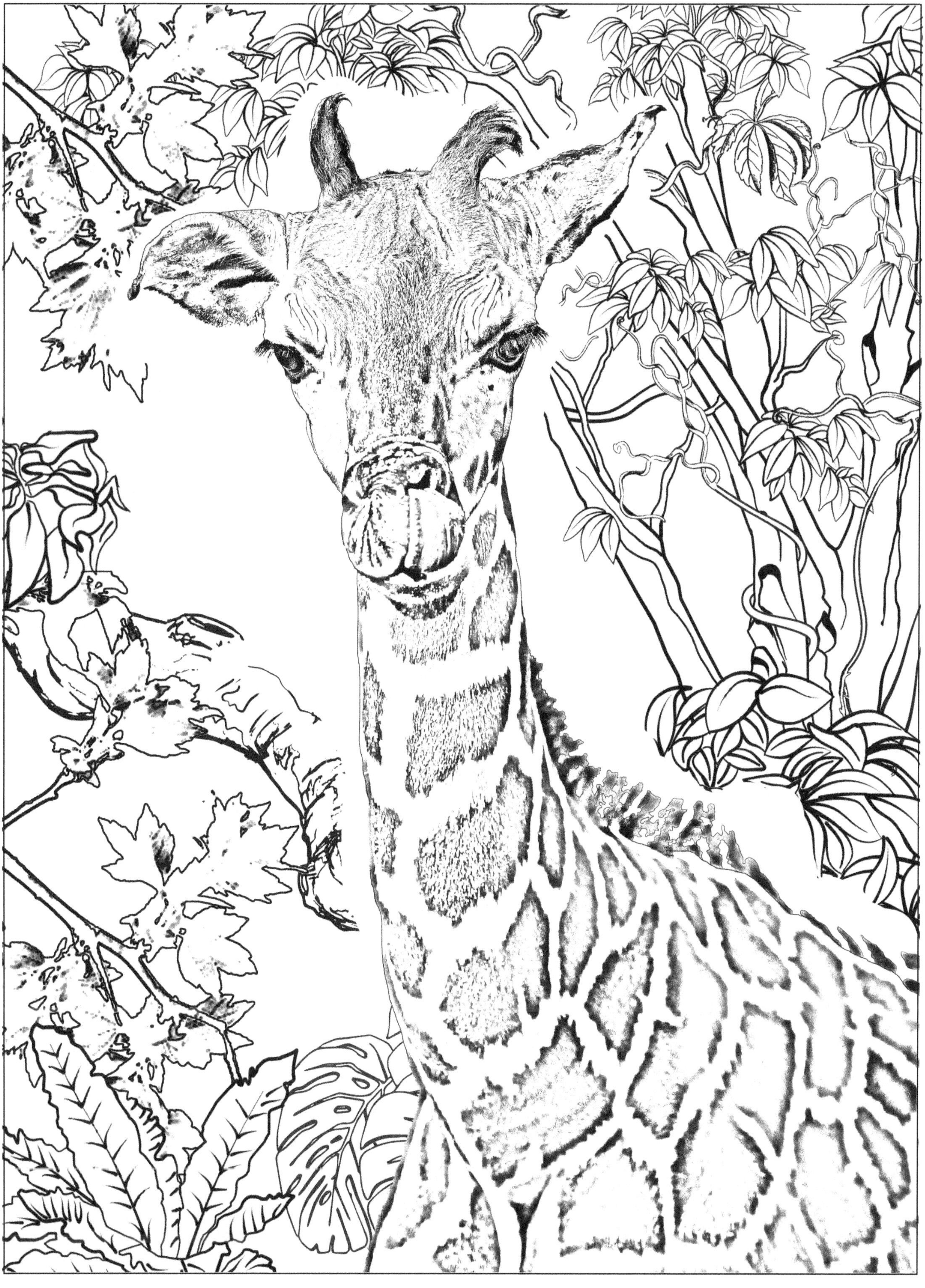

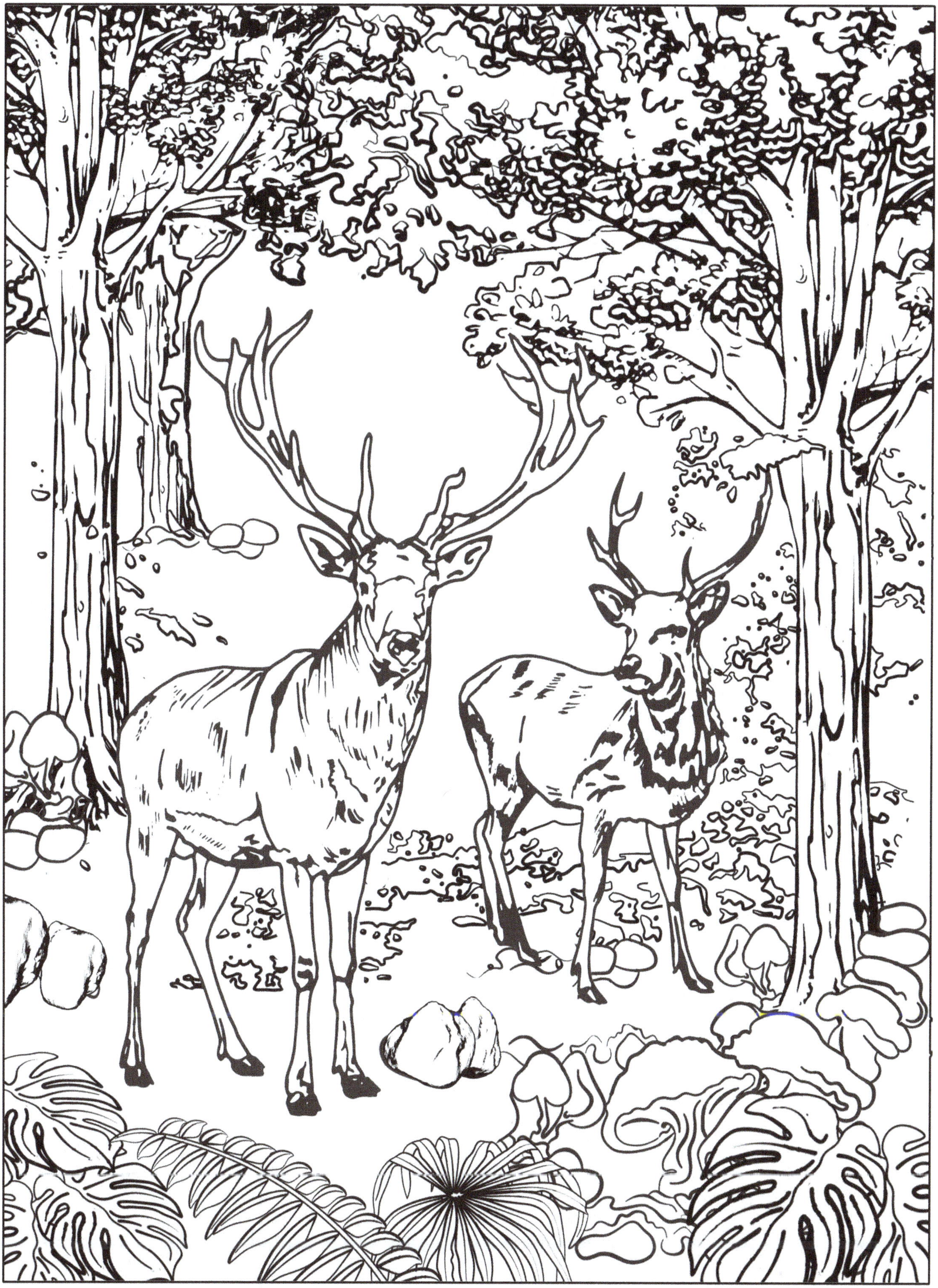

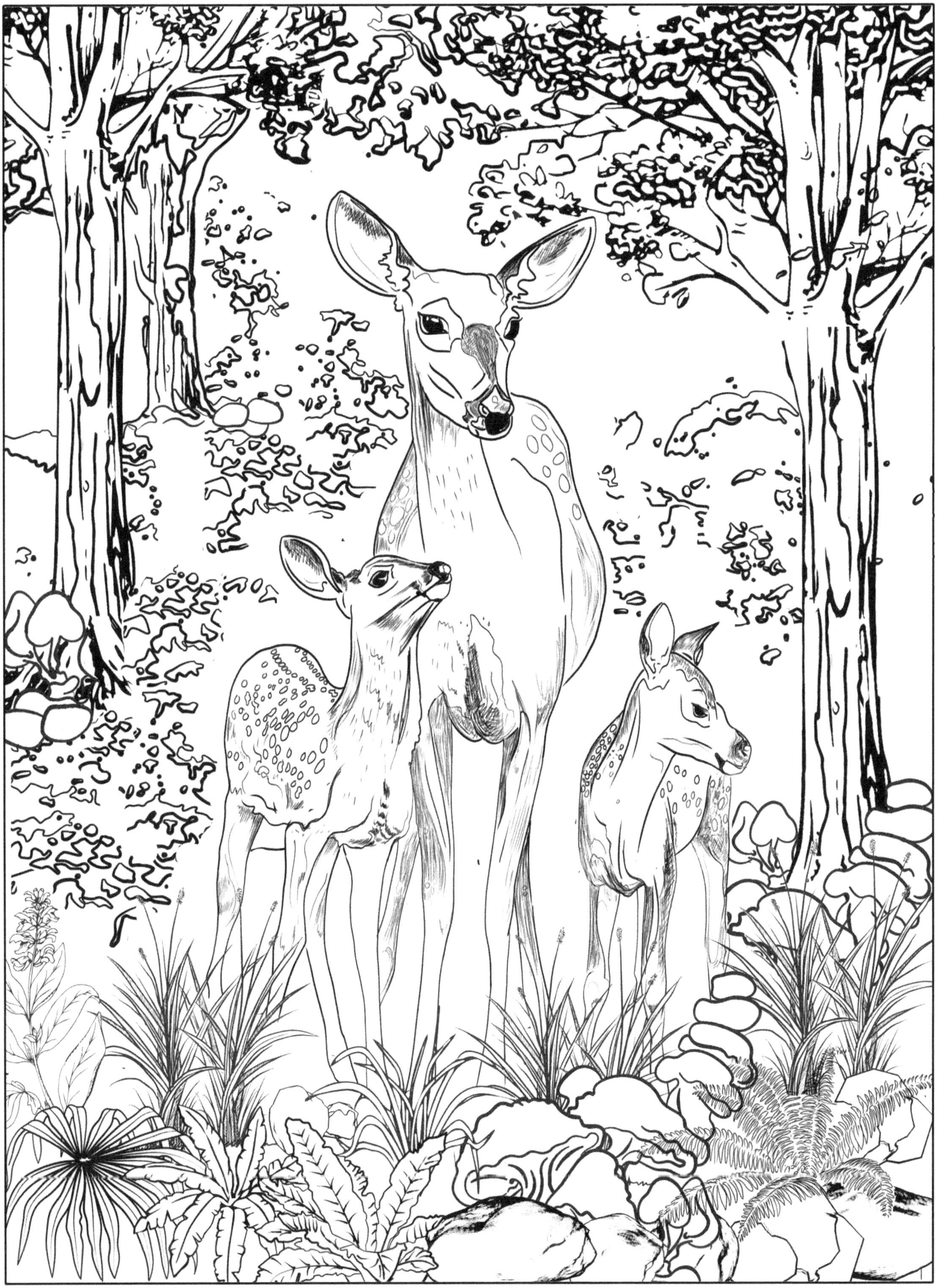

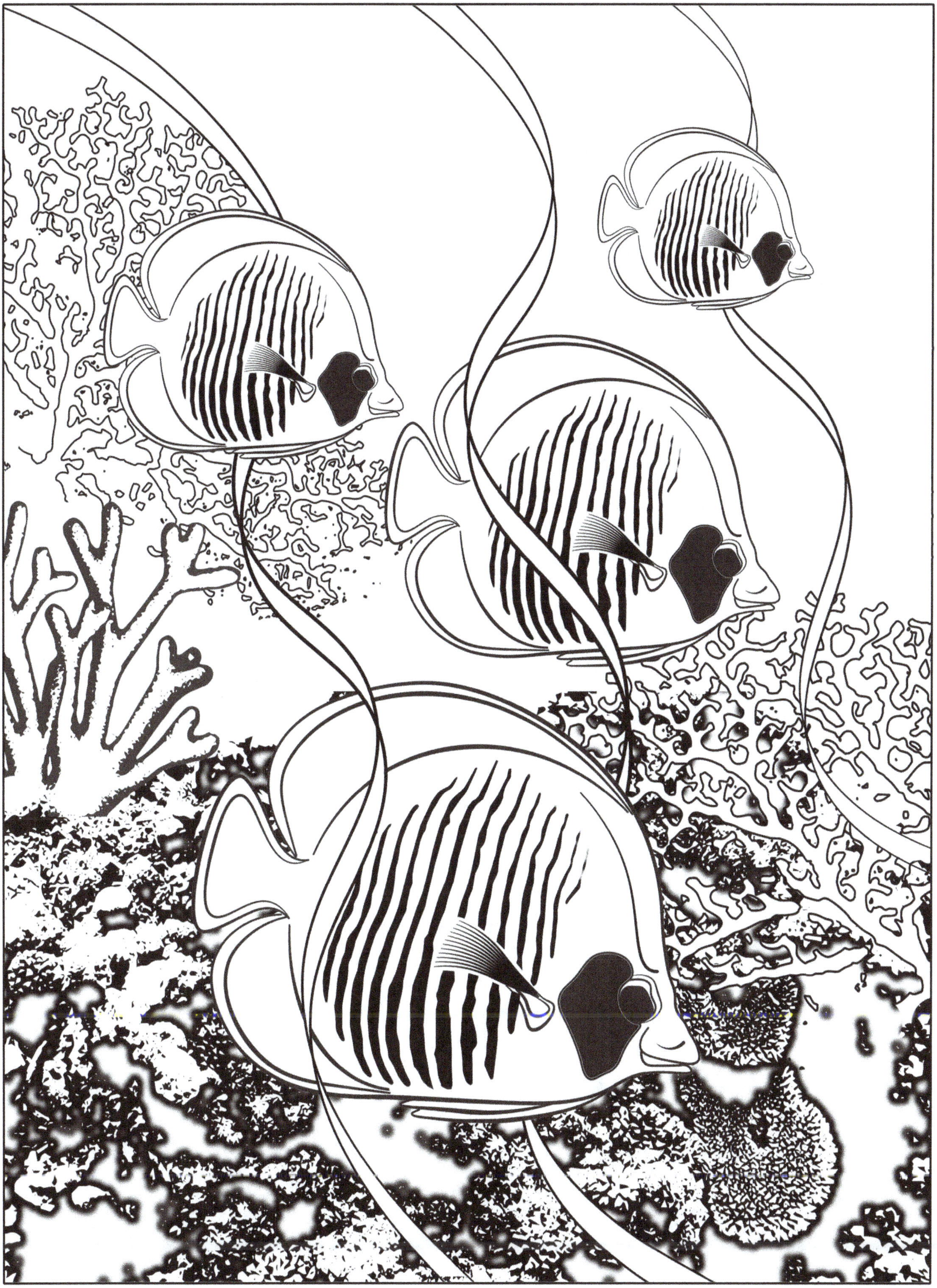

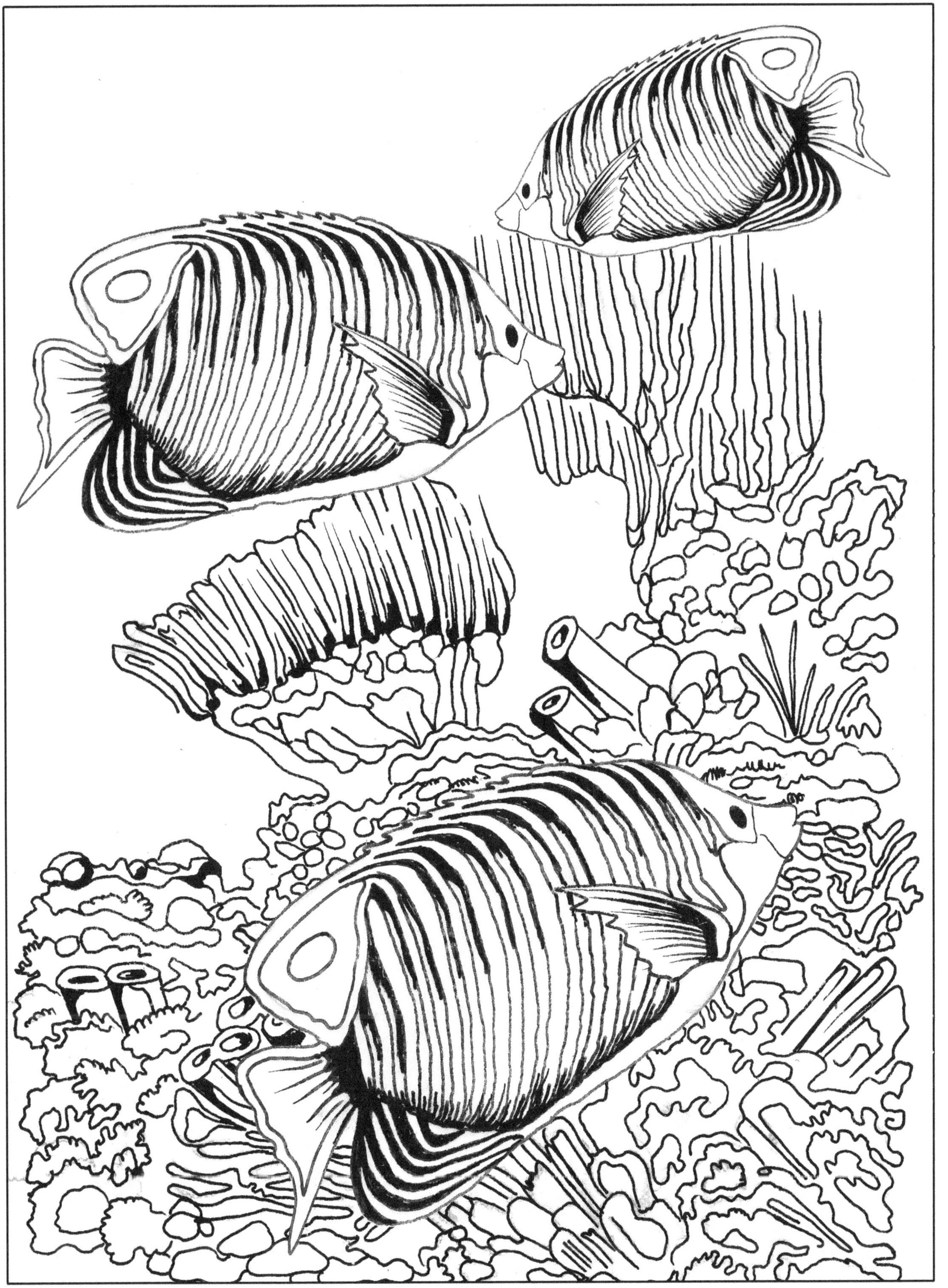

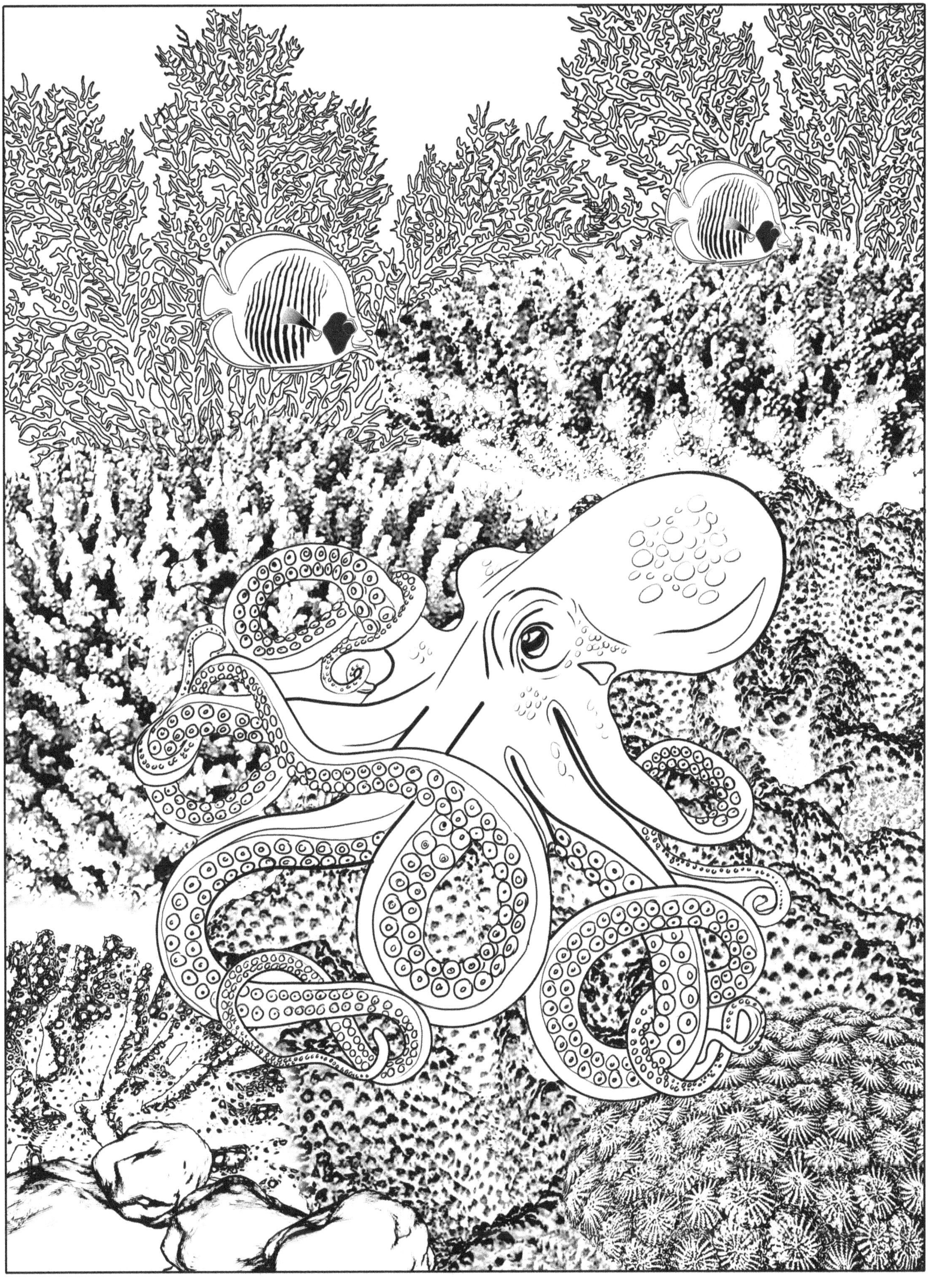

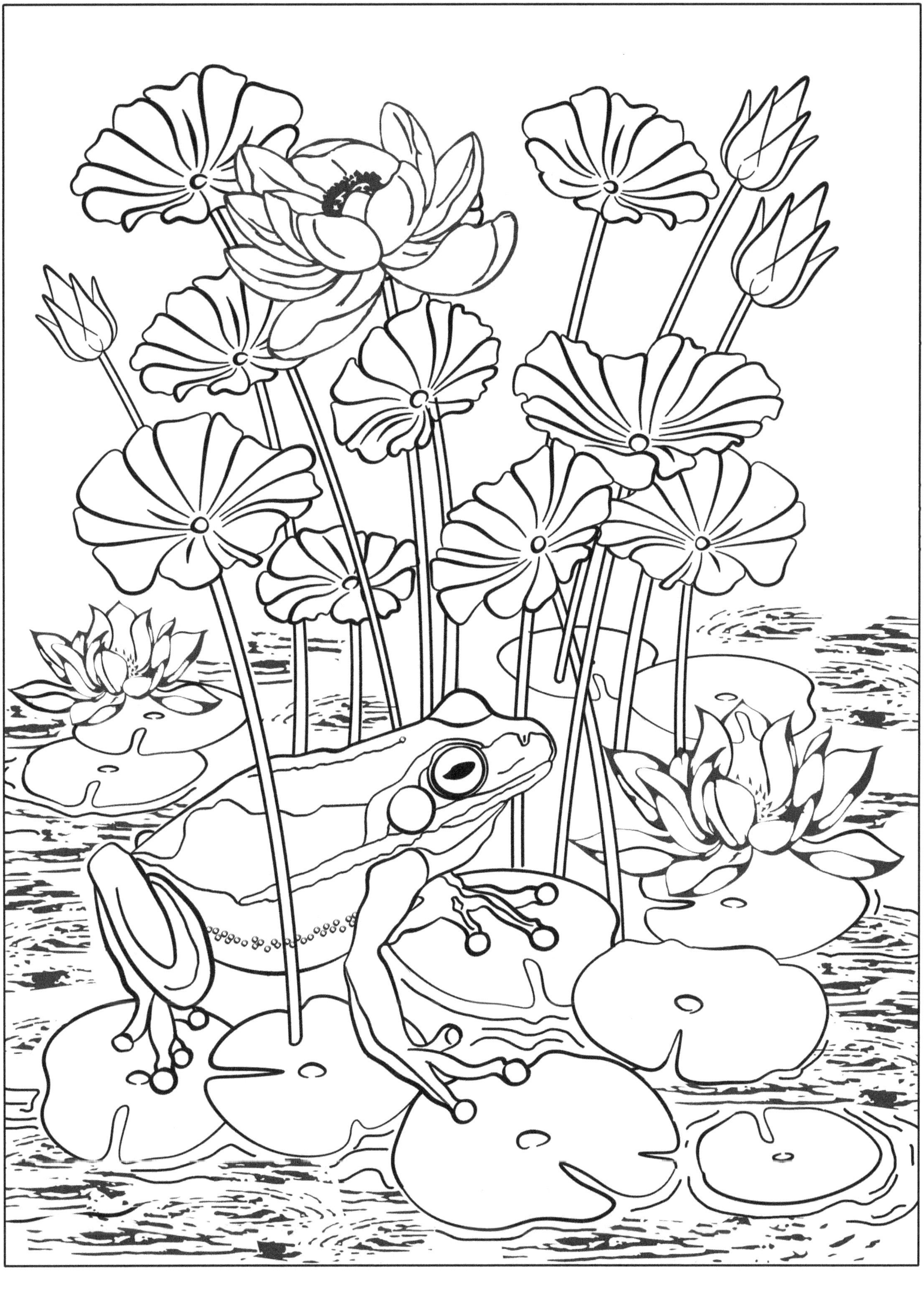

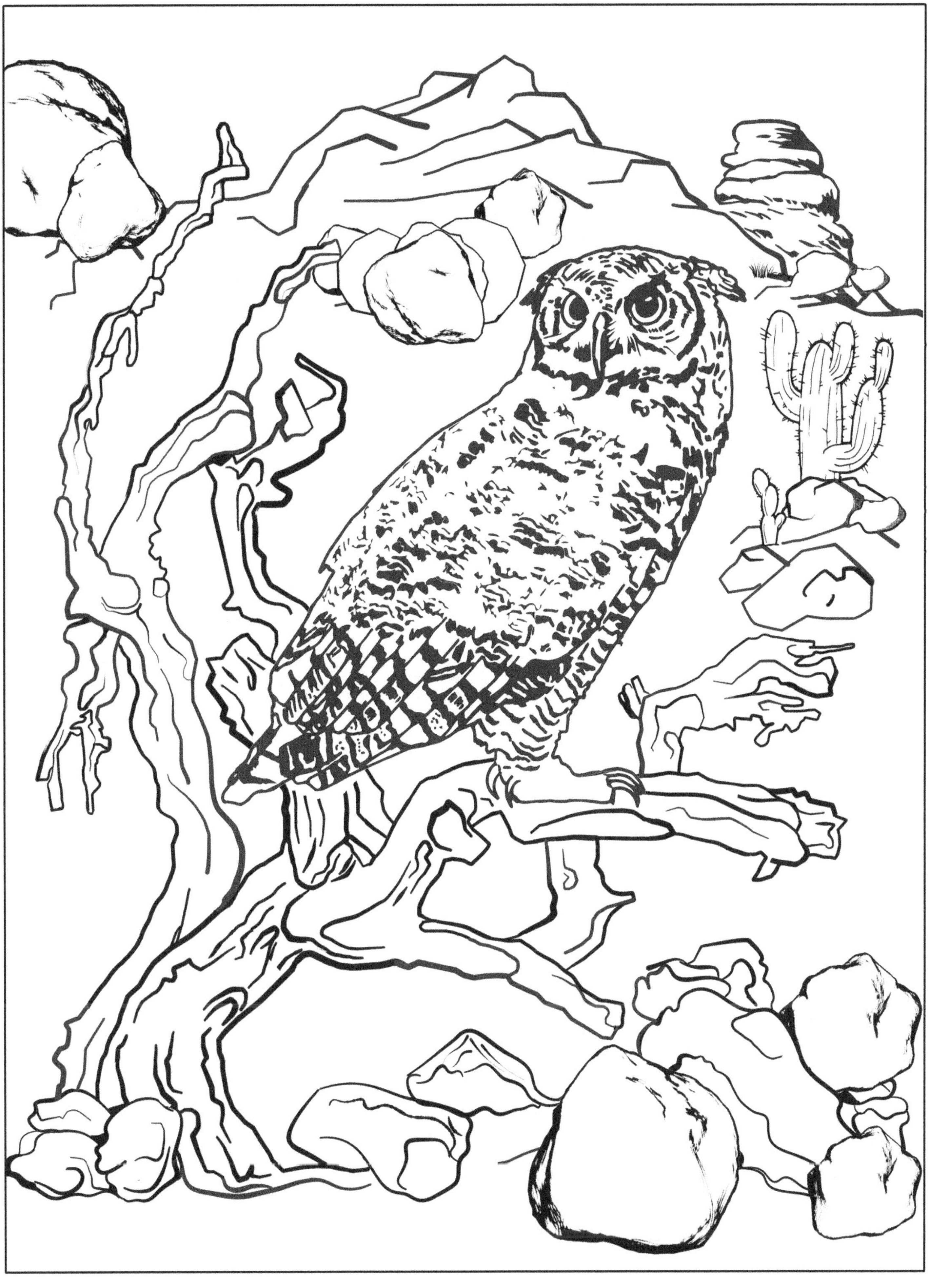

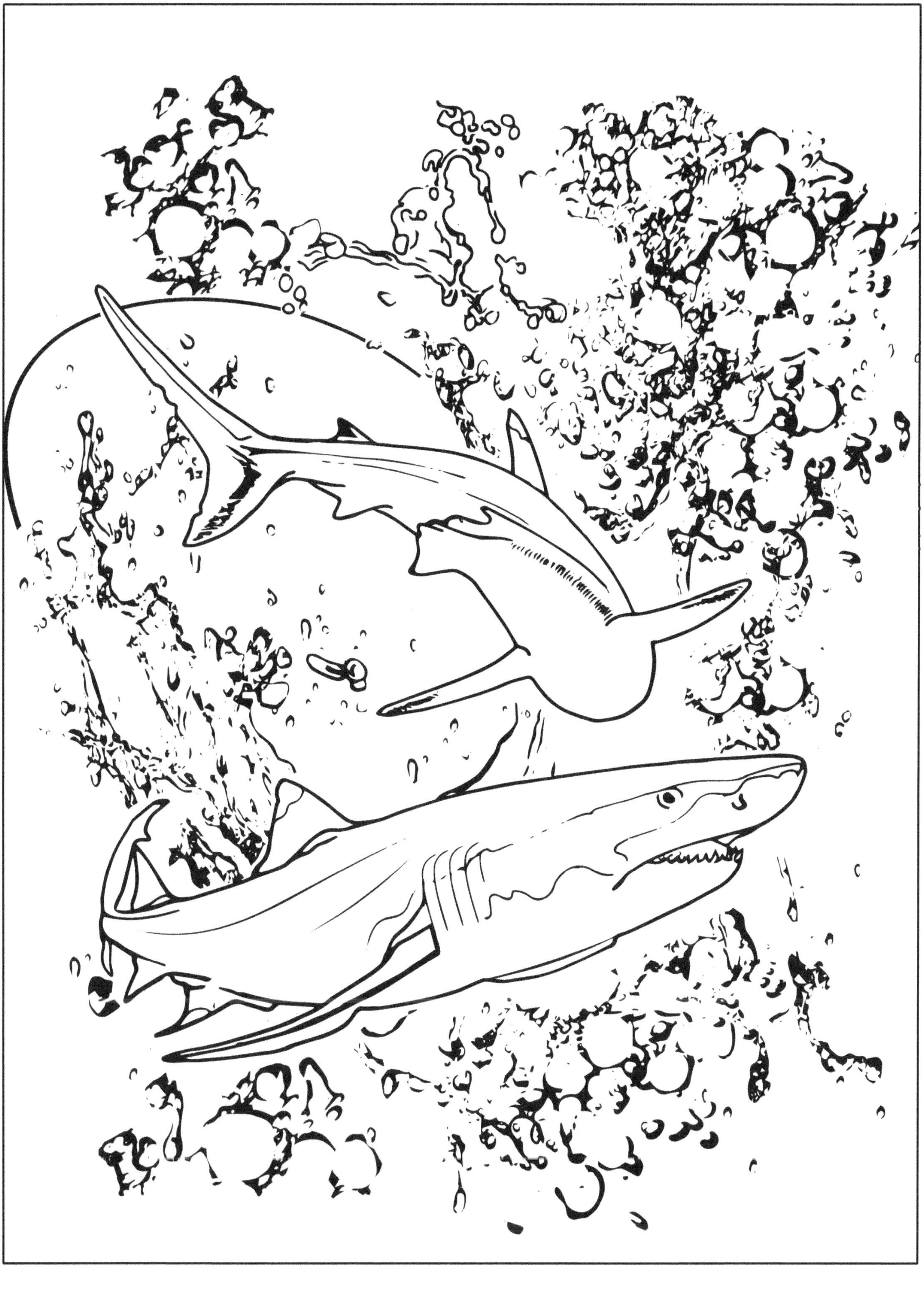

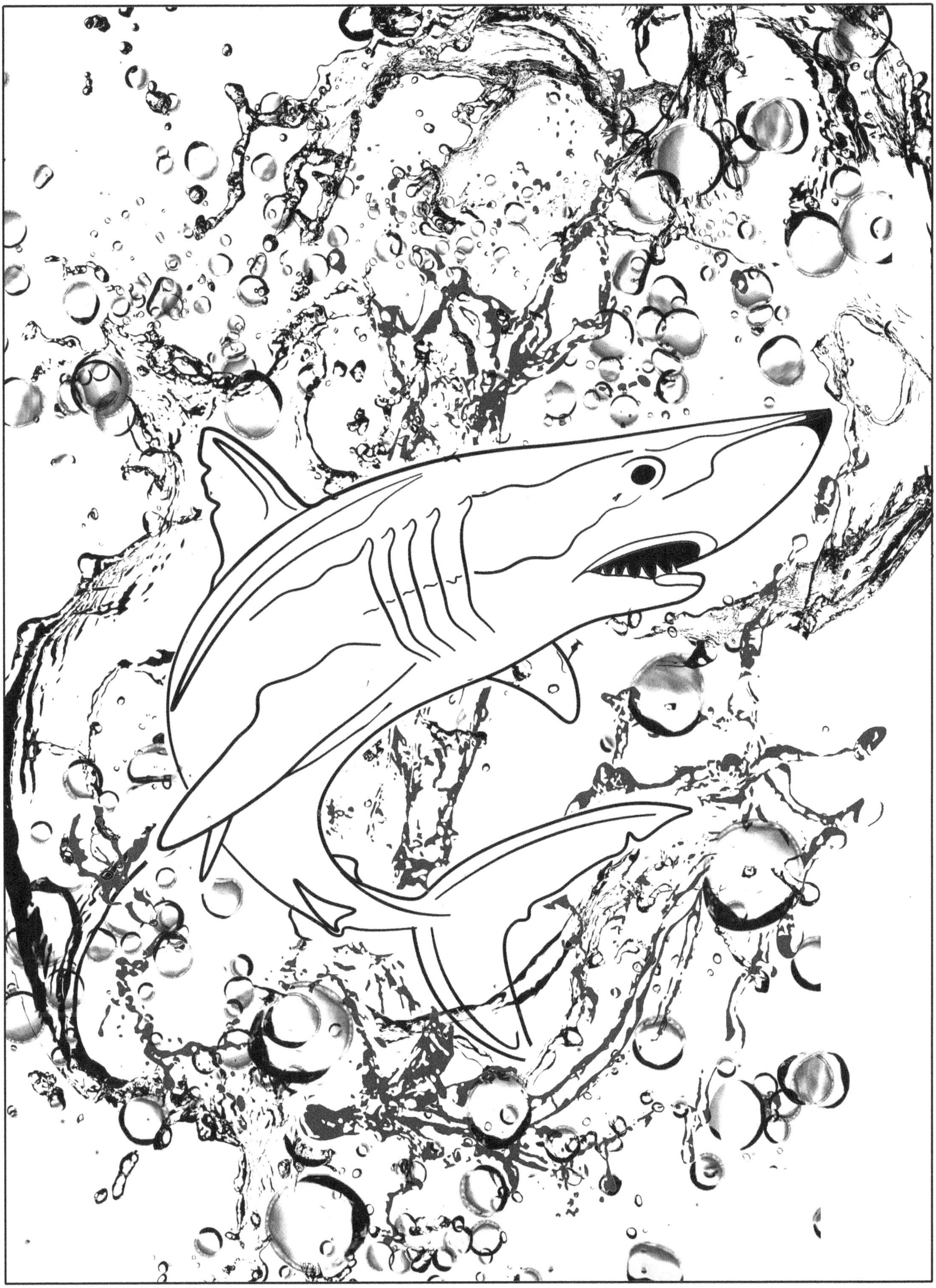

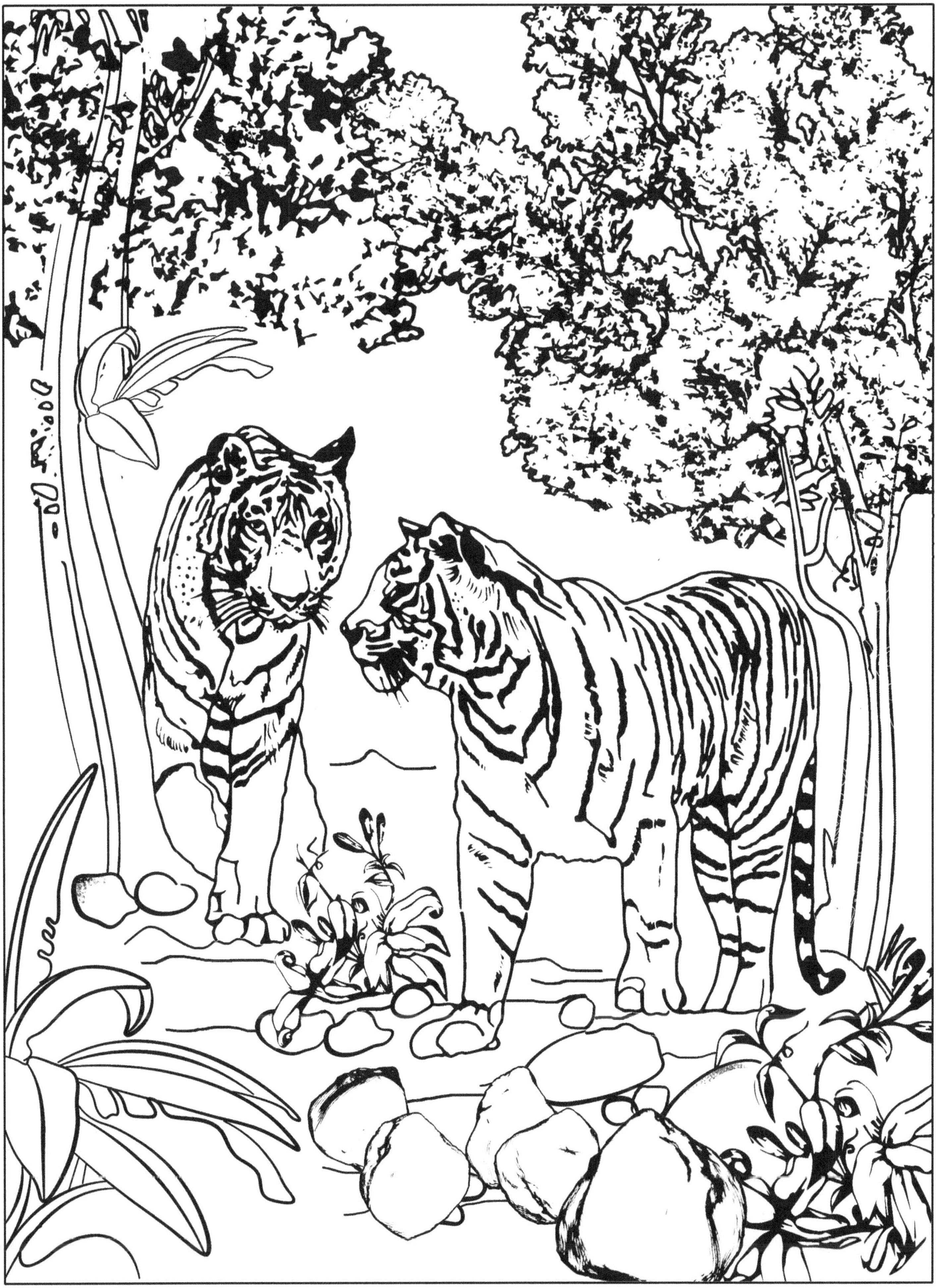

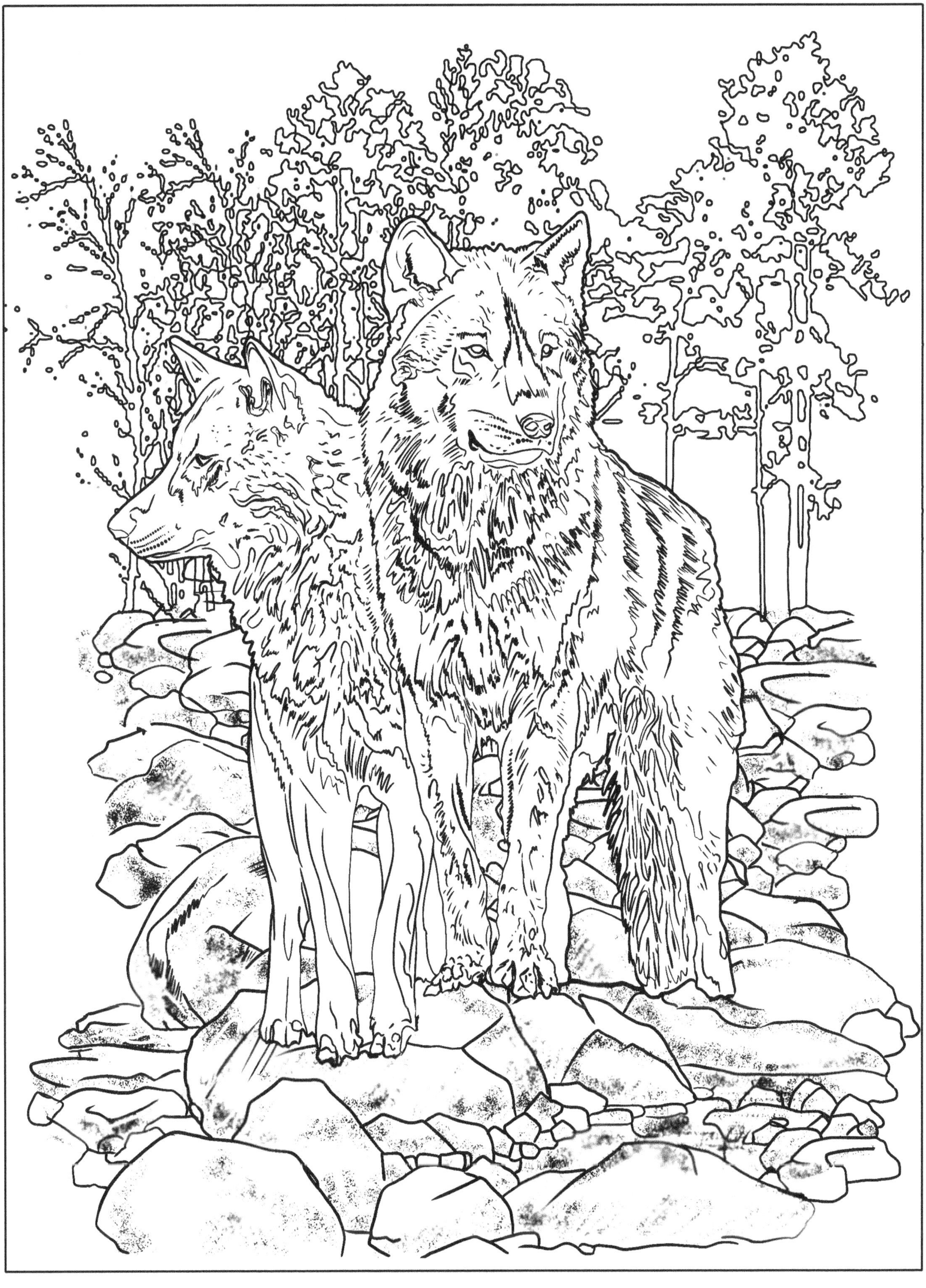

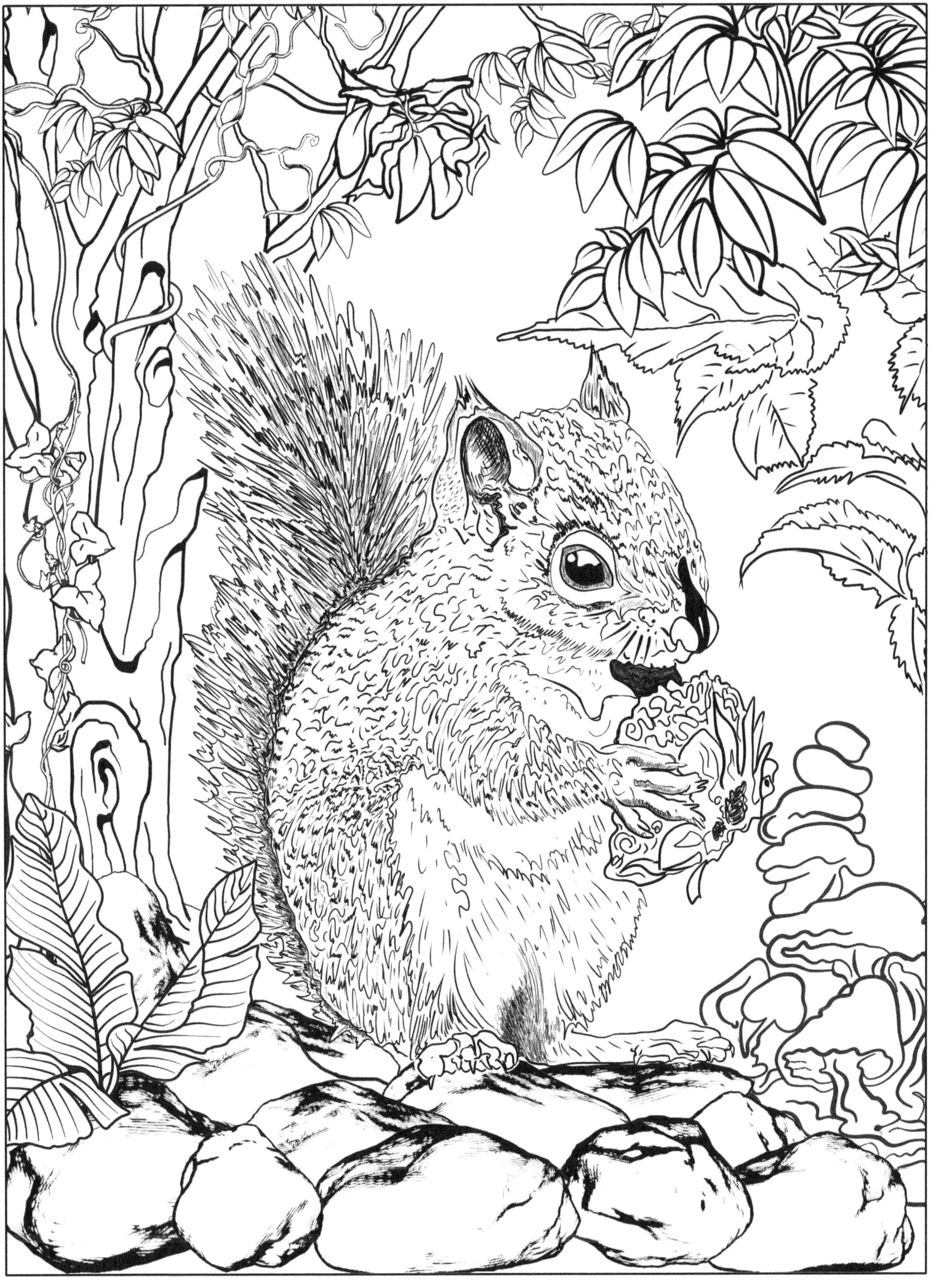

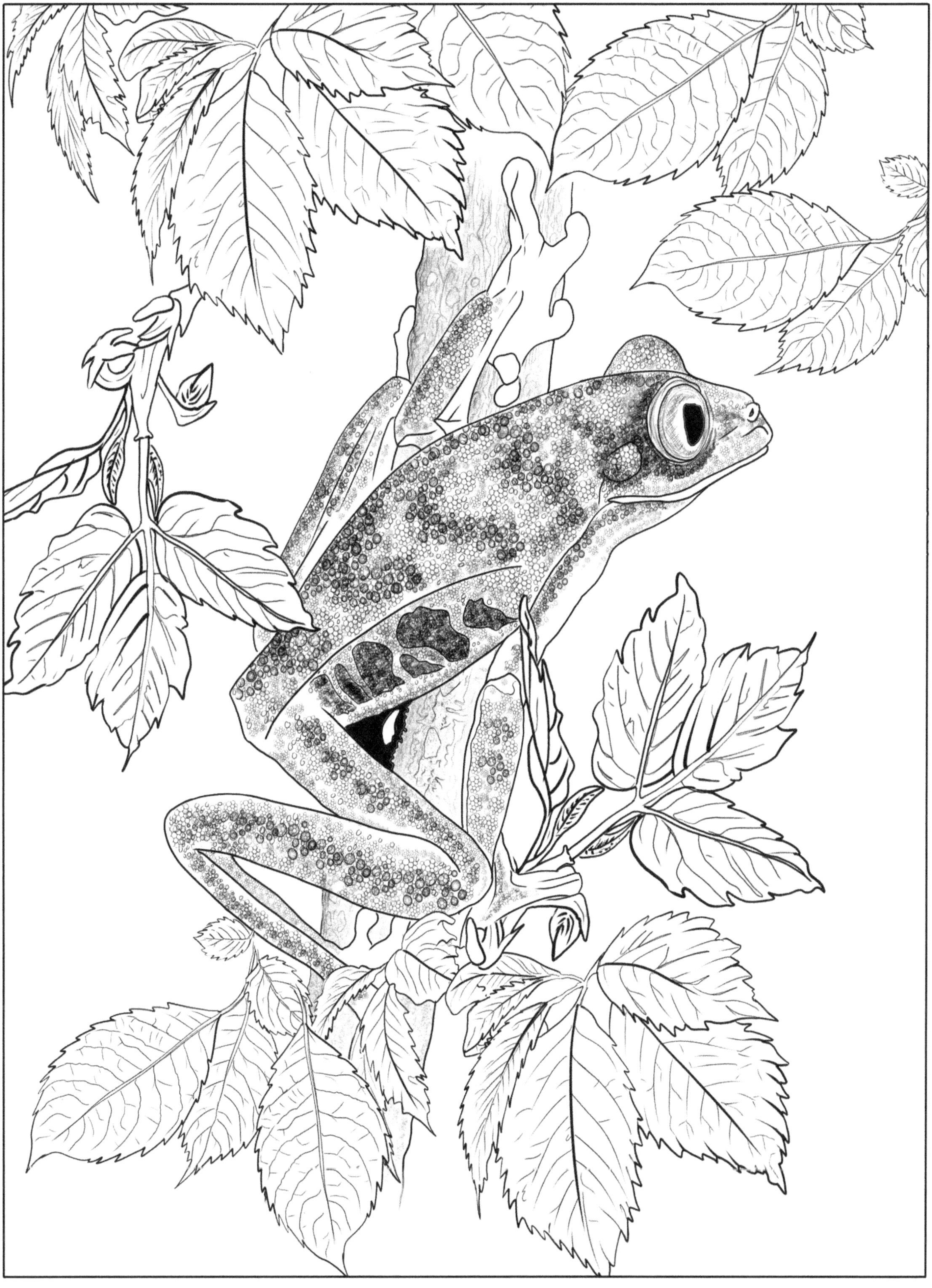

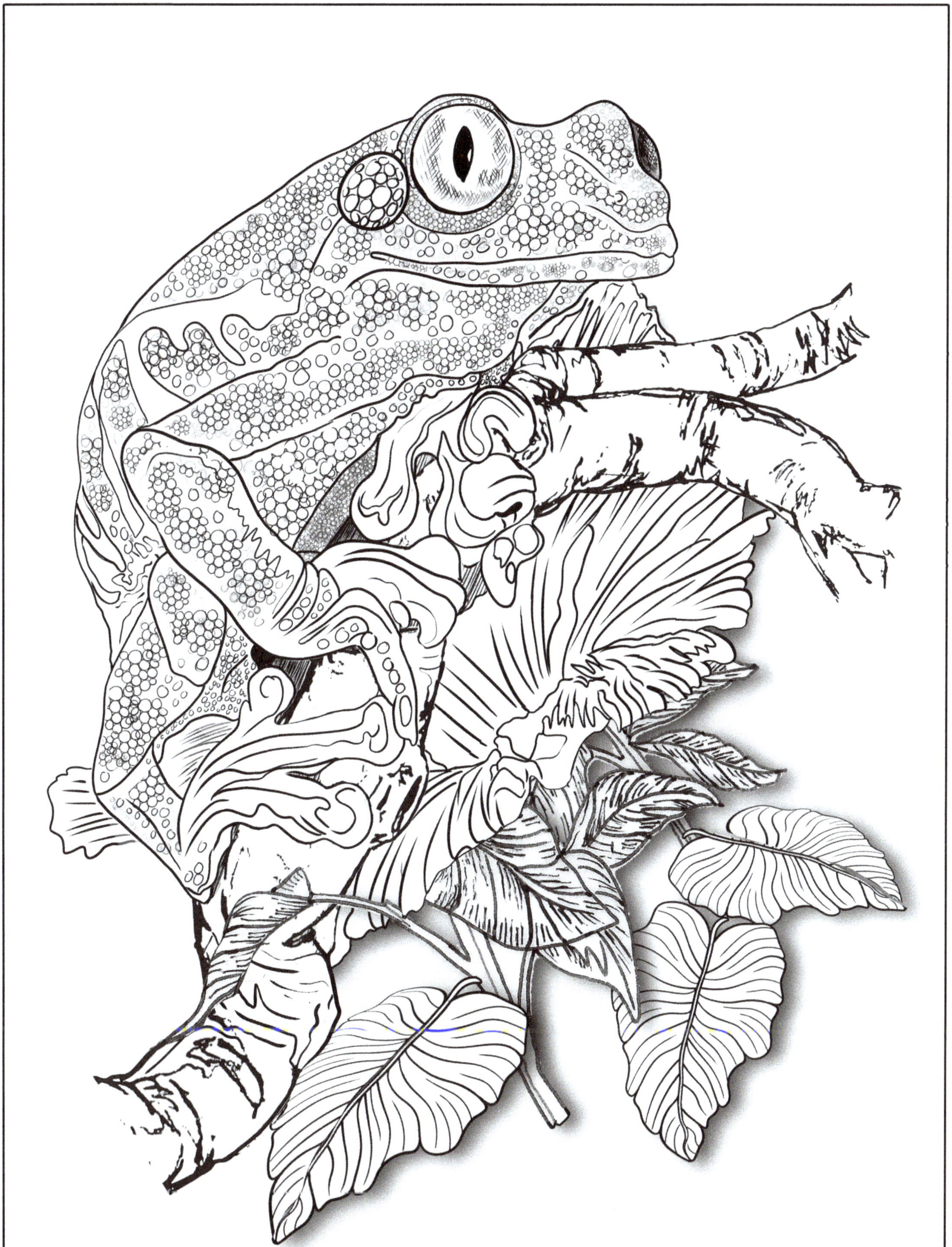

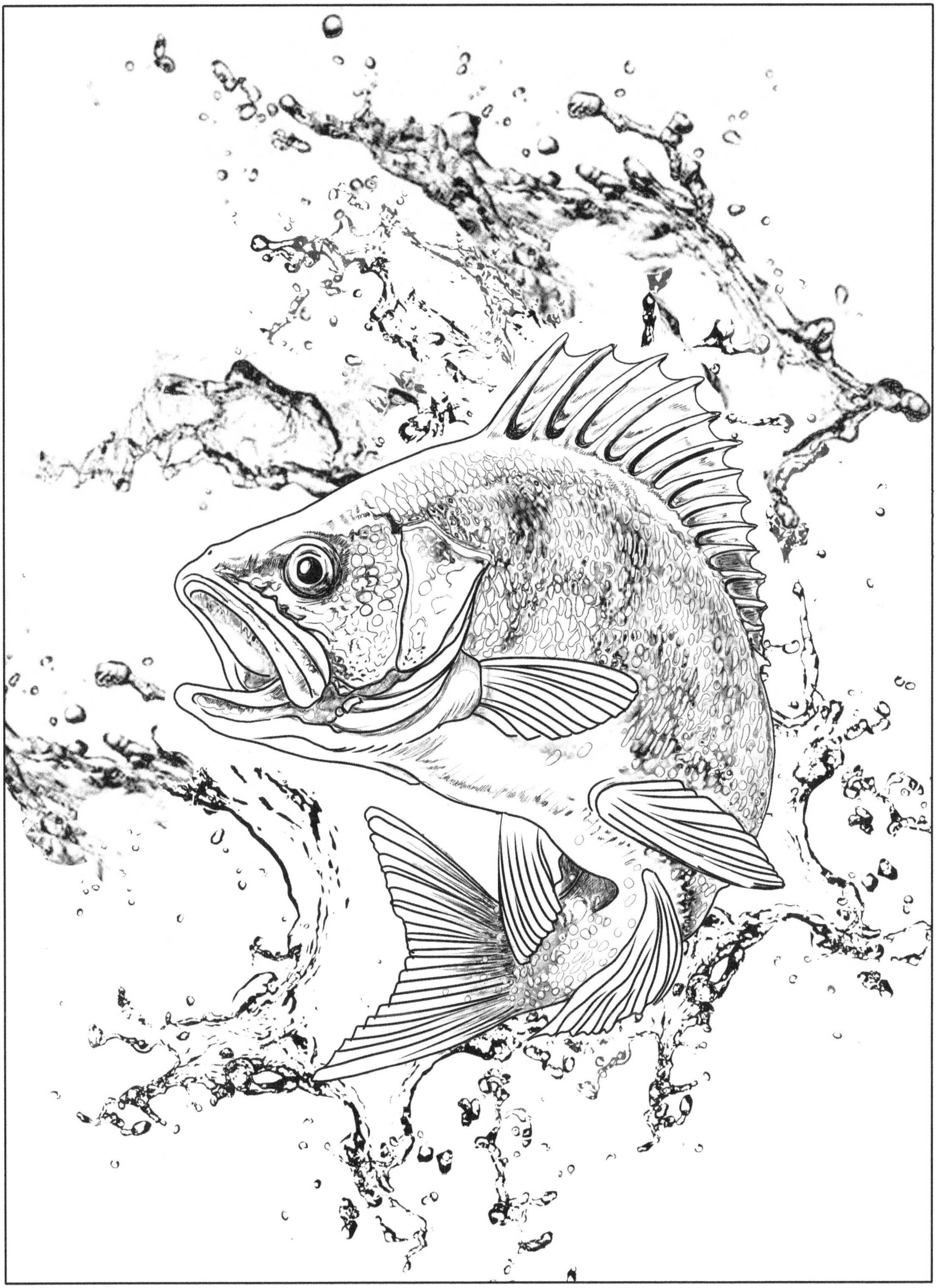

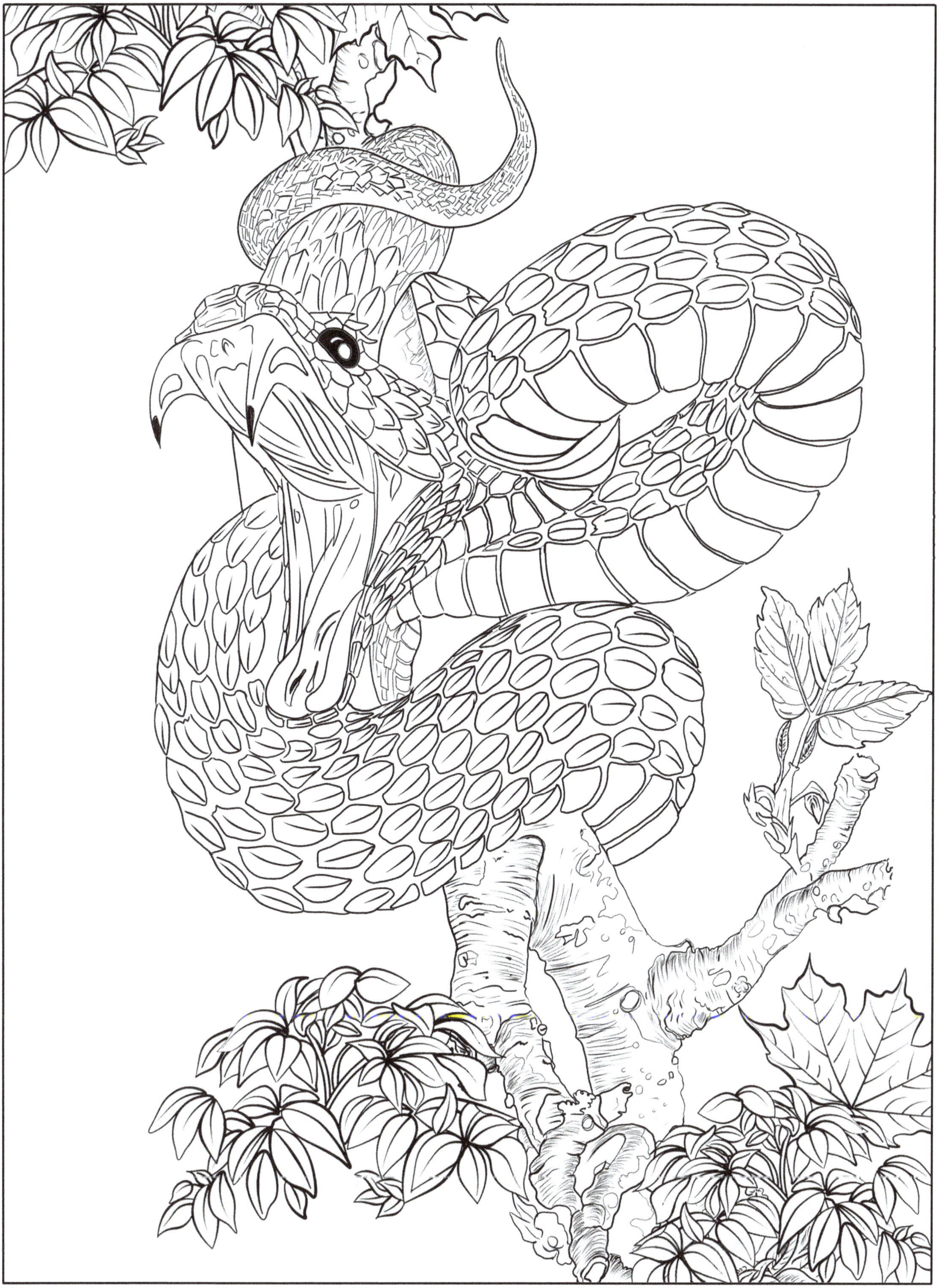

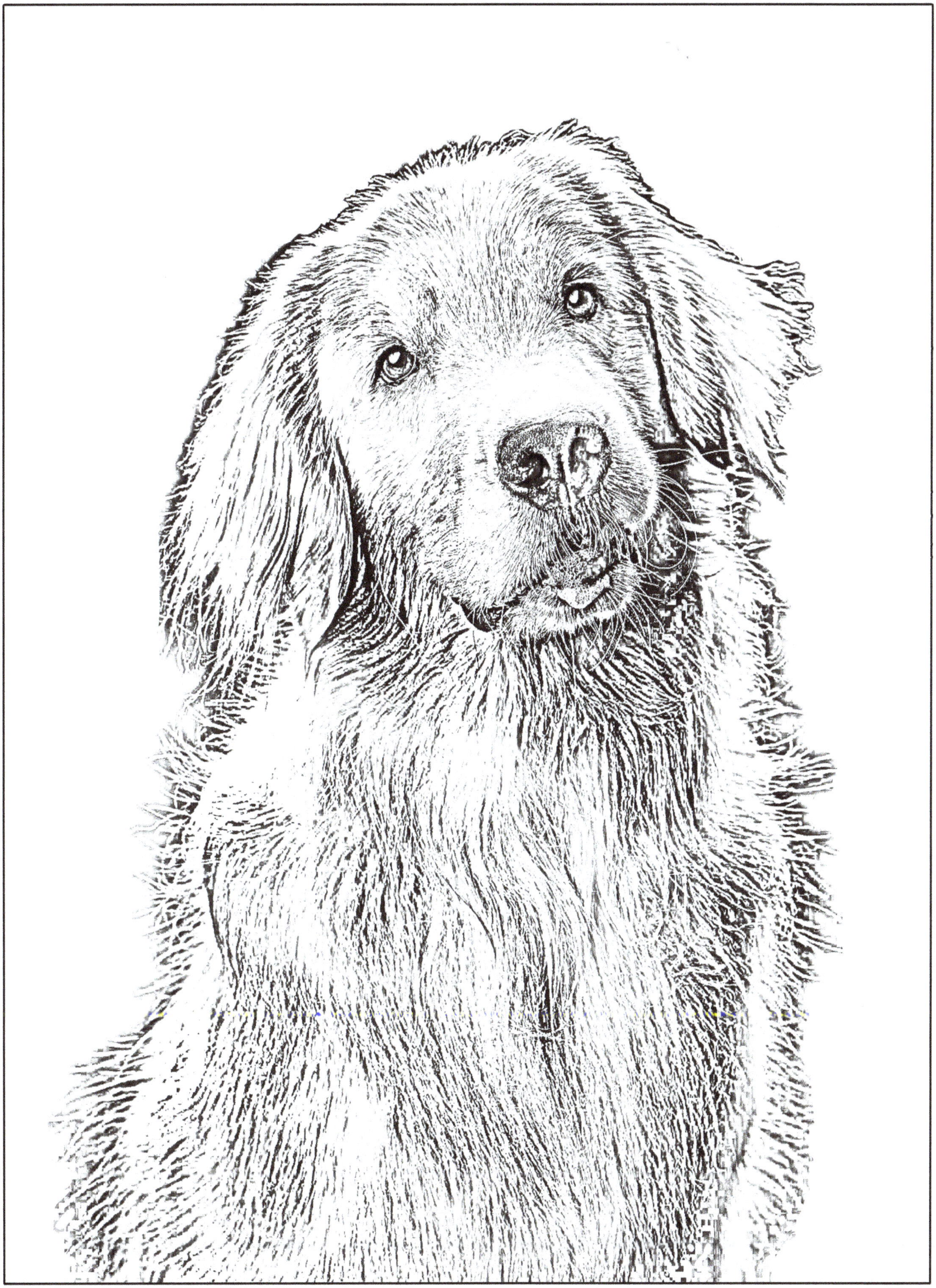

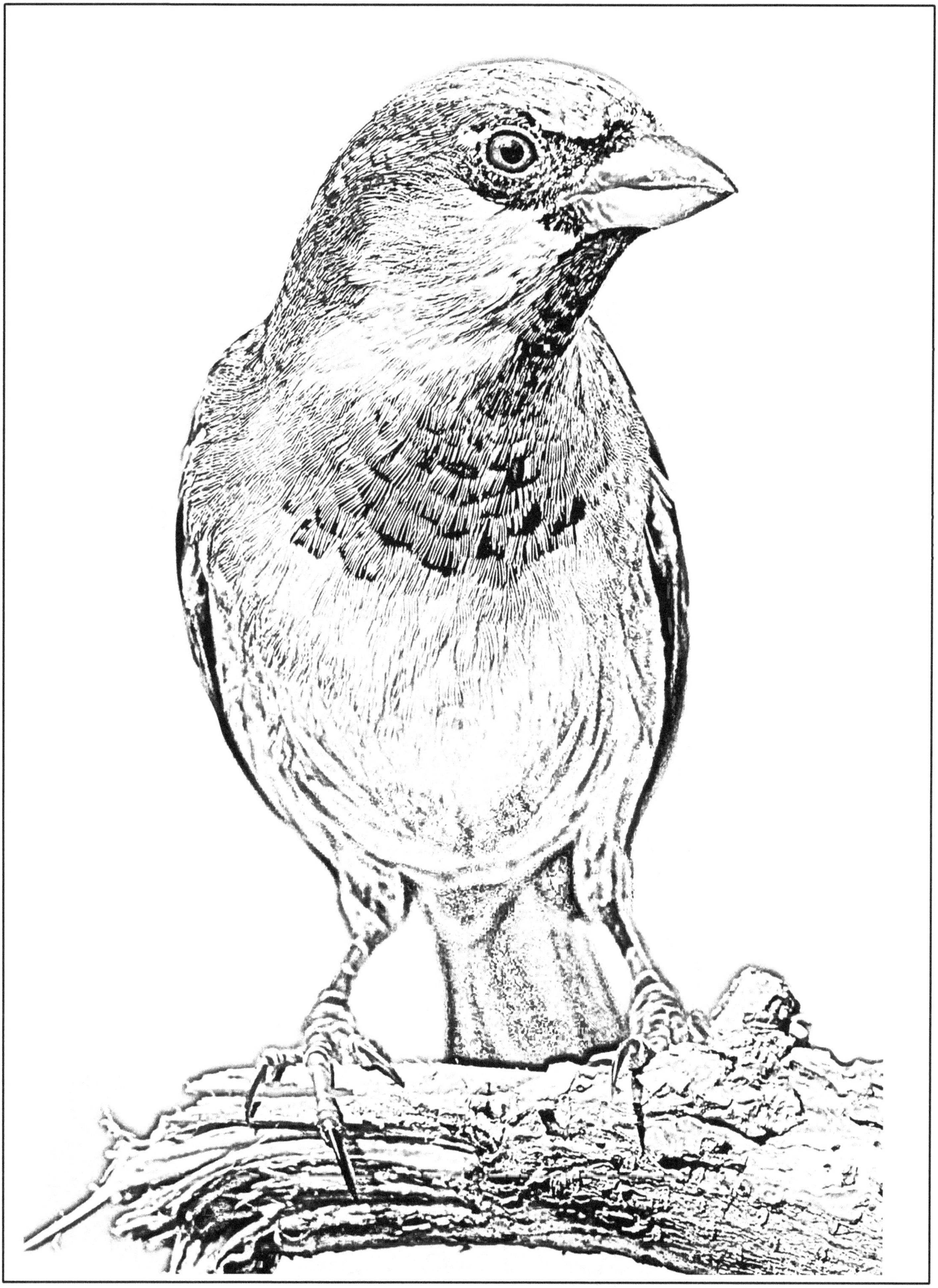

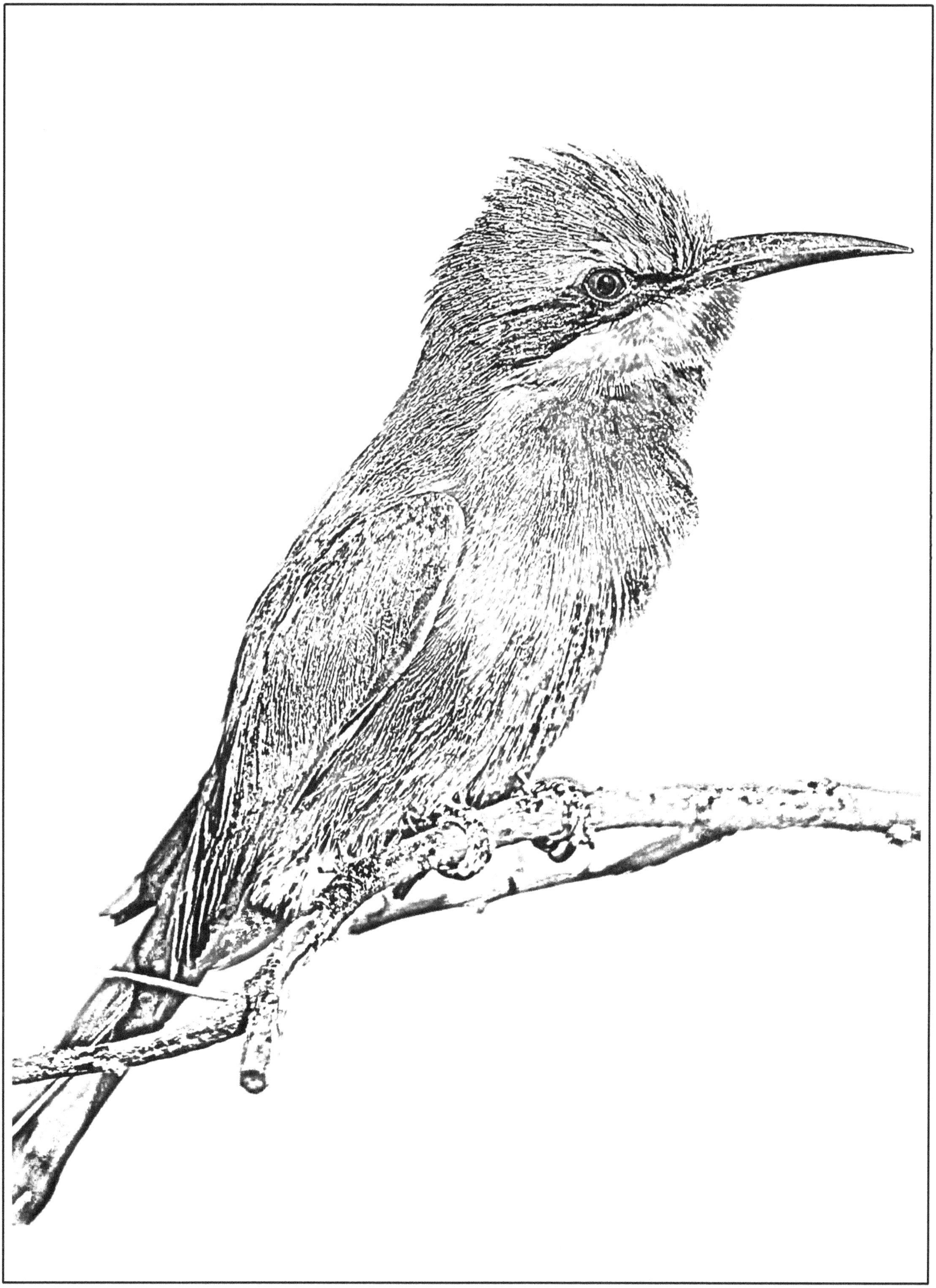

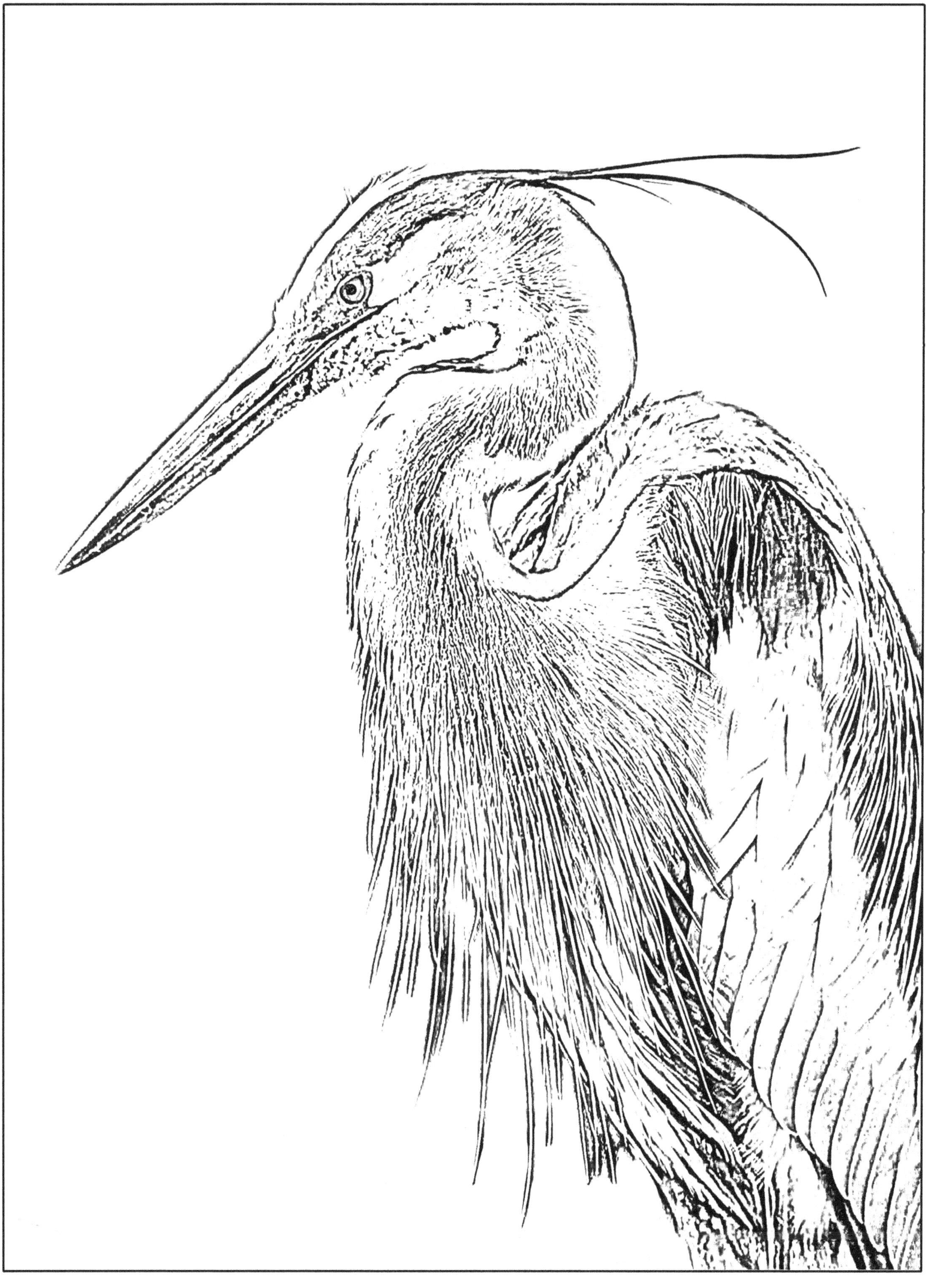

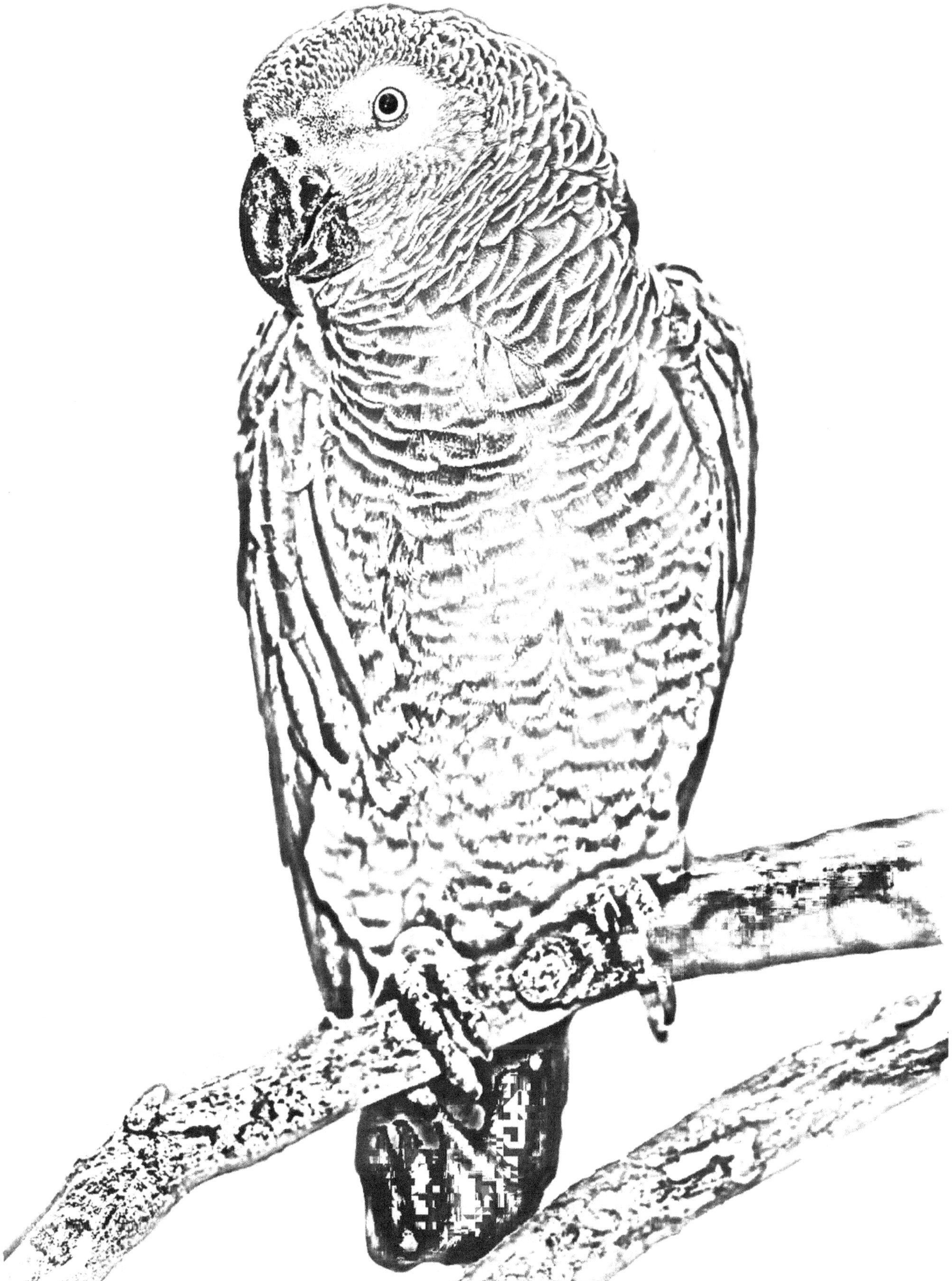

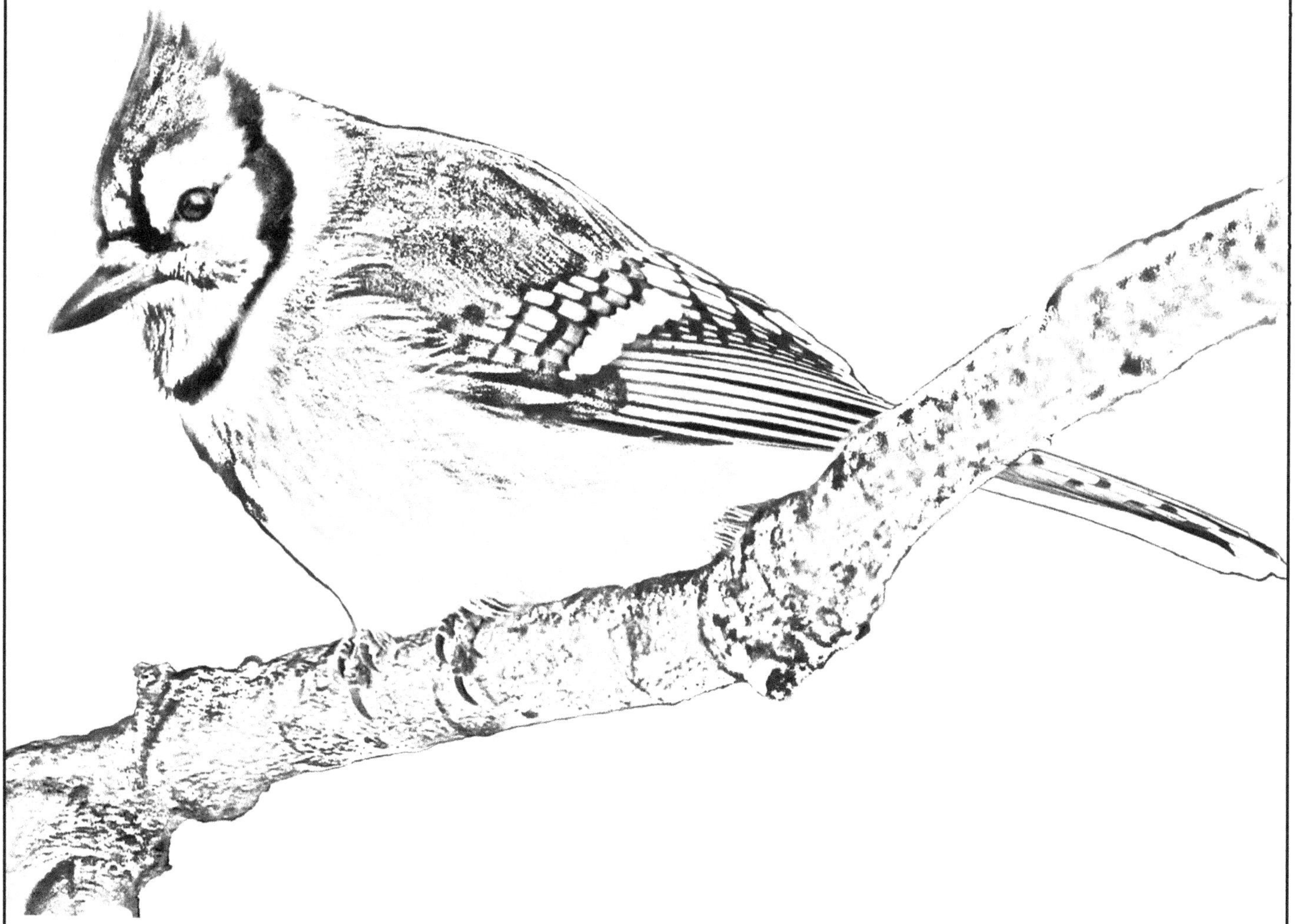

www.ingramcontent.com/pod-product-compliance
Lightning Source LLC
Chambersburg PA
CBHW081533220526
45467CB00010B/3177
* 9 7 8 1 7 0 5 5 9 6 8 3 8 *